# CHORD PROGRESSIONS
# THEORY AND PRACTICE

EVERYTHING YOU NEED TO CREATE AND USE
CHORDS IN EVERY KEY

DAN FOX • DICK WEISSMAN

Alfred Music
P.O. Box 10003
Van Nuys, CA 91410-0003
alfred.com

ISBN-10: 0-7390-7056-8
ISBN-13: 978-0-7390-7056-7

# Contents

# Foreword

Chord progressions are the building blocks that define the structure of music. Any intermediate keyboard player or other musician familiar with the grand staff is ready to learn about chords with *Chord Progressions: Theory and Practice*.

This book provides an easy way to create and use chords in any style of music, and it is divided into four sections. In Section 1, we establish the nature of chords, starting with simple major chords, and progress to more complex chords, involving additional notes.

In Section 2, we begin to deal with how chords are used and modified in contemporary music. At the same time, we show how chords can be simplified. This is especially important when playing with guitarists. While pianists play with 10 fingers and can change chords at the drop of a hat, this is a more complex process for guitarists.

Section 3 explores the way chord progressions indicate or even define musical styles. You will learn progressions in rock, pop, blues, swing, bebop, and many more popular styles.

Section 4 introduces advanced chord substitutions to spice up any progression.

By using this book, you will gain an enhanced understanding of the role of chords, and the way chord progressions and chord substitutions are used in a variety of musical styles.

*Dan Fox and Dick Weissman*

# Section I
# Chords, Intervals, and Scales

In this section, we cover how to understand and create simple and complex chords. By the end, you'll know what notes are contained in every possible chord in every practical key. You'll understand triads, 6ths, 7ths, 9ths, 11ths, and 13ths—all of which are described in detail. You will also know about suspensions, altered chords, and power chords, and how they are used in today's music. In addition, we discuss intervals and scales. There is also a chart of every practical major chord to refer back to at any time.

## Overview: Chords, Intervals, Scales, and Triads

### Chords

*Chords* consist of at least three different notes that can be played simultaneously or separately. For example: C–E–G or G–B–D–F. The name of the chord is determined by its most important note, the *root*. Examples: The root of a C chord is the note C. The root of a G7 chord is the note G.

#### Chord Progressions

A *chord progression* is a series of chords played one after the other. A progression begins on a certain chord, goes through other different chords, and almost always returns to the first chord. A very simple example is a progression that starts with the C chord, moves to the G7, chord and then returns to the C chord.

#### Chord Symbols

A *chord symbol* consists of one or two parts. The first part is a capital letter that tells you what the root of the chord is. For example: C, G, F♯, B♭, etc. If the symbol has no second part, the chord is a *major chord*. For example, C means "C major chord," B♭ means "B♭ major chord," and so on. If the chord is not a major chord, the second part of the chord symbol gives a brief description of the quality of the chord. For example, G7 means "G seventh chord." B♭m means "B♭ minor chord" and so on. We'll give you more details a little later in this book.

#### Slash Marks

The sign / is called a *slash mark*. It means to repeat the previous chord. For example, C / / / means to play the C chord four times—once for the chord symbol (C) and once each for the slash marks.

#### Building Chords

Before you can build chords, it is important to understand the major scale and the intervals that make up that scale.

## Intervals

The distance between two notes is an *interval*.

### Intervals of a Half Step

From any key on the piano to the next key (black or white) is a *half step*. On guitar, a half step is the distance between any fret and the next fret on the same string. The half steps are C to C♯ (or D♭); C♯ (or D♭) to D; D to D♯ (or E♭); D♯ (or E♭) to E; E to F; F to F♯ (or G♭); F♯ (or G♭) to G; G to G♯ (or A♭); G♯ (or A♭) to A; A to A♯ (or B♭); A♯ (or B♭) to B (or C♭); B (or C♭) to C. When there are two names for the same note, such as C♯ and D♭, the notes are called *enharmonic equivalents*.

### Intervals of a Whole Step

The distance from any key on the piano to two keys away (black or white) is a *whole step*. On guitar, a whole step is two frets away on the same string (for example, the 3rd and 5th frets are a whole step apart). The whole steps are C to D; C♯ (or D♭) to D♯ (or E♭); D to E; D♯ (or E♭) to F; E to F♯ (or G♭); F to G; F♯ (or G♭) to G♯ (or A♭); G to A; G♯ (or A♭) to A♯ (or B♭); A to B (or C♭); A♯ (or B♭) to C; B (or C♭) to C♯ (or D♭).

## Major Scales

A *major scale* consists of eight notes that occur in alphabetical order. The last note has the same name as the first note but is an *octave* (eight notes) higher. There is a pattern of whole (W) and half (H) steps that you use to create all major scales: W–W–H–W–W–W–H. For example, the C major scale consists of the notes C–D–E–F–G–A–B–C.

### C Major Scale

The G major scale has the notes G–A–B–C–D–E–F♯–G.

### G Major Scale

In all, there are 15 practical major scales. They can be found on pages 6 and 7.

### Scale Steps

If you look at the scales on pages 6 and 7, you'll notice there is a number below each note. These numbers show what step in the scale the note represents. For example, the note C is the first note in the C scale, so it has a 1 below it. The note D is the second note, so it is numbered 2. The note G is the fifth note and is numbered 5, and so on. These numbers are very important in understanding how chords are constructed.

# Major Scales

### C Major

Scale steps: 1       2       3       4       5       6       7       8

### C♯ Major

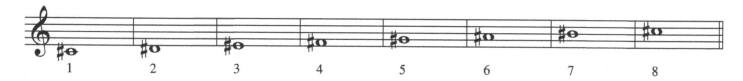

1       2       3       4       5       6       7       8

### D♭ Major

1       2       3       4       5       6       7       8

### D Major

1       2       3       4       5       6       7       8

### E♭ Major

1       2       3       4       5       6       7       8

### E Major

1       2       3       4       5       6       7       8

### F Major

1       2       3       4       5       6       7       8

**F♯ Major**

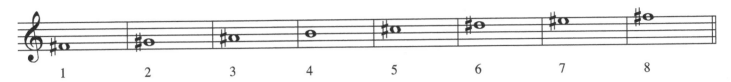

1  2  3  4  5  6  7  8

**G♭ Major**

1  2  3  4  5  6  7  8

**G Major**

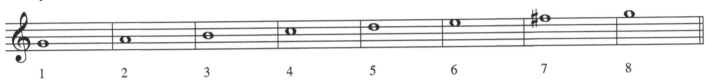

1  2  3  4  5  6  7  8

**A♭ Major**

1  2  3  4  5  6  7  8

**A Major**

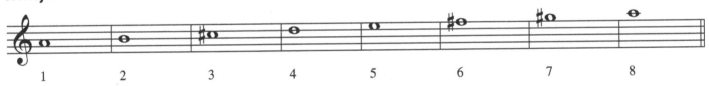

1  2  3  4  5  6  7  8

**B♭ Major**

1  2  3  4  5  6  7  8

**B Major**

1  2  3  4  5  6  7  8

**C♭ Major**

1  2  3  4  5  6  7  8

# Triads

A *triad* is a chord consisting of three different notes that may be played in any order. For example, C–E–G, C–G–E, G–C–E, and E–G–C are all C major triads. Also, any note may be played more than once. For example, C–E–G–C, C–G–E–C–E, and C–E–G–C–E–G are all C major triads. There are five kinds of triads in common use: *major, minor, diminished, augmented,* and *suspended*.

### Major Triads

The symbol for a major triad is simply a capital letter, sometimes with an accidental, for example: C, G, F#, B♭. To build a major triad, choose the 1, 3, and 5 of any major scale. For example, the notes in a C major triad are found in the C major scale: 1 (C), 3 (E), and 5 (G). Using a G major scale, the notes of a G major triad are 1 (G), 3 (B), and (5) D. The B♭ triad is spelled B♭–D–F. The F# major triad is spelled F#–A#–C#.

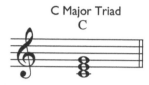

### Minor Triad

The symbol for a minor triad is either a small "m" or "min." If you see Cm or Cmin, say "C minor." To build the chord, select the 1, 3, and 5 of any major scale, then lower the 3rd by a half step. For example, the C major chord is C–E–G; the C minor chord is C–E♭–G. The E♭ major chord is E♭–G–B♭; the E♭ minor chord is E♭–G♭–B♭. If the 3rd is a sharped note, lower it to a natural. For instance, the D major chord is D–F#–A so the D minor chord is D–F–A. If the 3rd is already flat, a double flat must be used. For instance, the G♭ major is G♭–B♭–D♭ so G♭ minor is G♭–B♭♭–D♭.

### Diminished Triad

The symbol for diminished is either "dim" or a small circle (°). If you see Cdim or C°, say "C diminished triad." In this case, it's a good idea to say the word "triad" to distinguish this chord from the C diminished 7th (see page 10) which is used more often. To build this chord, select the 1, 3, and 5 from any major scale. Then, lower both the 3rd and the 5th by a half step each. For instance, C major = C–E–G so C dim. = C–E♭–G♭; D major = D–F#–A so D dim.= D–F–A♭. Like in the minor chord, if a note is already flat, technically, the double flat ♭♭ should be used. Practically, however, it's better to spell the chord the easiest way. For example, D♭ major = D♭–F–A♭. Technically, D♭dim should be spelled D♭–F♭–A♭♭, but practically, it's better to spell it enharmonically as D♭–E–G.

### Augmented Triad

The symbol for an augmented triad is either "aug" or a small plus sign +. If you see Caug or C+, say "C augmented." To build this chord, select 1, 3, and 5 from any major scale, and then raise the 5 one half step. For example, C major = C–E–G so C aug. = C–E–G#. If the 5th is flat, it becomes a natural: D♭ major = D♭–F–A♭ so D♭+ = D♭–F–A. If the 5th is already sharp it becomes a double sharp ×. For example, B major = B–D#–F# so B+ = B–D#–F×. Here again, it's usually better to simplify the spelling enharmonically as B–D#–G.

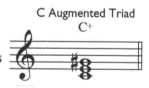

### Major Chord with Suspended 4th

The symbol for this chord is either "sus4" or simply "sus." Select the 1, 4, and 5 of any major scale. For example, Csus4 = C–F–G; Esus4 = E–A–B; G♭sus4 = G♭–C♭–D♭; and so on. This chord is very common in contemporary music.

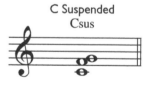

# Four-Note Chords

Four-note chords are expansions of the triads you have already learned. When notes are added to chords, it adds new sounds, or colors, to the music you are playing.

## Chords Built on the Major Triad

There are three basic four-note chords built on the major triad.

### Major 7th chord

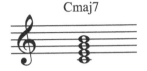
Cmaj7

Symbols: maj7, M7, or △7.
Start with a major triad (1–3–5) and add the 7.
*Examples:*
Cmaj7=**C**–**E**–**G**–B; Gmaj7=**G**–**B**–**D**–F♯;
G♭maj7=**G♭**–**B♭**–**D♭**–F; and so on.

### Dominant 7th chord (usually called a "seventh chord")

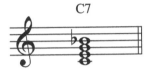
C7

Symbol: 7
Start with a major triad (1–3–5) and add a flatted 7th.
*Examples:*
For C7, start with the C major triad and add the flatted 7th (B♭); C7=**C**–**E**–**G**–B♭. For E♭7, start with the E♭ major triad and add the flatted 7th (D♭); E♭7=**E♭**–**G**–**B♭**–D♭. For E7, start with the E major triad and add the flatted 7th (D natural); E7=**E**–**G♯**–**B**–D.

### Major 6th chord (usually called a "sixth chord")

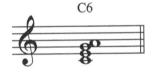
C6

Symbol: 6 or maj.6
Start with a major triad (1–3–5) and add a 6th.
*Examples:*
C6=**C**–**E**–**G**–A; G6=**G**–**B**–**D**–E.
E♭6=**E♭**–**G**–**B♭**–C; F♯6=**F♯**–**A♯**–**C♯**–D♯.

## Chords Built on the Minor Triad

As you've already learned the minor triad contains the 1–♭3–5 of the major scale. Here are basic four-note chords built on minor triads:

### Minor/Major 7th chord

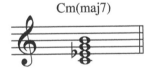
Cm(maj7)

Symbol: m(maj7), m+7, or min maj7
Start with a minor triad (1–♭3–5) and add the 7.
*Examples:*
Cm(maj7)=**C**–**E♭**–**G**–B. Gm(maj7)= **G**–**B♭**–**D**–F♯. E♭m(maj7)=**E♭**–**G♭**–**B♭**–D.
Bm(maj7)=**B**–**D**–**F♯**–A♯.

### Minor 7th chord

Cm7

Symbol: m7 or min7
Start with a minor triad (1–♭3–5) and add a flatted 7th.
*Examples:*
Cm7=**C**–**E♭**–**G**–B♭; Gm7=**G**–**B♭**–**D**–F;
Em7=**E**–**G**–**B**–D; D♭m7=**D♭**–**F♭**–**A♭**–C♭.

### Minor 6th chord

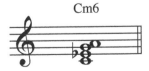
Cm6

Symbol: m6 or min6
Start with a minor triad (1–♭3–5) and add the 6.
*Examples:*
Cm6=**C**–**E♭**–**G**–A; Gm6=**G**–**B♭**–**D**–E;
B♭m6=**B♭**–**D♭**–**F**–G; F♯m6=**F♯**–**A**–**C♯**–D♯.

## Chords Built on the Diminished Triad

The same three notes (7, ♭7, and 6) that we added to major and minor triads can be added to the diminished triad as follows:

### Diminished with added major 7th

Cdim+7

Symbol: °+7 or dim+7
Start with the diminished triad (1–♭3–♭5) and add the 7.
   *Examples:* Cdim+7=**C–E♭–G♭**–B.
   G°+7=**G–B♭–D♭**–F♯. F♯dim+7=**F♯–A–C**–E♯. E♭°+7=**E♭–G♭–B♭♭**–D (with easier
      spelling E♭–F♯–A–D)

### Half-diminished 7th (also known as a minor 7♭5)

C<sup>ø</sup>7

Symbol: <sup>ø</sup>7, m7(♭5)
Start with the diminished triad (1–♭3–♭5) and add ♭7.
   *Examples:*
   C<sup>ø</sup>7=**C–E♭–G♭**–B♭; F<sup>ø</sup>7=**F–A♭–C♭**–E♭;
   E<sup>ø</sup>7=**E–G–B♭**–D; B♭<sup>ø</sup>7=**B♭–D♭–F♭**(E)–A♭

### Diminished 7th

C°7

Symbol: °7 or dim7
Start with the diminished triad (1–♭3–♭5) and add the 6 (technically, the ♭♭7).
   *Examples:*
   Cdim7=**C–E♭–G♭**–A; Gdim7=**G–B♭–D♭**–E; F♯dim7=**F♯–A–C**–E♭; B♭dim7=**B♭–D♭–E**–G.

> **Important:** Many modern arrangers use "dim" when they really mean "dim7." In general, unless the chord symbol specifies "dim triad," use the diminished 7th.

## Chords Built on the Augmented Triad

There are only two four-note chords built on the augmented triad.

### Major 7th Sharp 5

Cmaj7(♯5)

Symbol: maj7(♯5), maj7+5, or maj7♯5
Start with the augmented triad (1–3–♯5) and add the 7.
   *Examples:* Cmaj7(♯5)=**C–E–G♯**–B;
   Gmaj7(♯5)=**G–B–D♯**–F♯; Dmaj7(♯5)=**D–F♯–A♯**–C♯; A♭maj7(♯5)=**A♭–C–E**–G

### Augmented 7th

C7(♯5)

Symbol: 7(♯5), 7+5, or 7♯5
Start with the augmented triad (1–3–♯5) and add a flatted 7.
   *Examples:*
   C7(♯5)=**C–E–G♯**–B♭; E♭7(♯5)=**E♭–G–B**–D♭; F♯7(♯5)=**F♯–A♯–C**(D)–E; A7(♯5)=**A–C♯–E♯**(F)–G.

## Chord Built on the Suspended Triad

There is only one four-note chord built on the suspended triad.

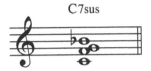

C7sus

### *Seventh Chord with Suspended 4th*

Symbol: 7sus or 7sus4

Start with the suspended triad (1–4–5) and add the flatted 7th;

*Examples:*

C7sus=**C–F–G–B**♭.

E♭7sus=**E♭–A♭–B♭–D**♭; F♯7sus=**F♯–B–C♯**–E; A7sus=**A–D–E**–G.

## Altered chords

Sometimes, chords are altered by lowering (flatting) the 5th of a four-note chord. Three common altered chords are:

### *Major 7th Flat 5*

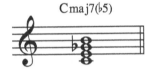

Cmaj7(♭5)

Symbol: maj7(♭5), maj7♭5, or maj7-5

Start with a major 7th chord and flat the 5th.

*Examples:*

**Cmaj7♭5**=C–E–G♭–B; **F♯maj7♭5**=F♯–A♯–C–E♯;

**E♭maj7-5**=E♭–G–B♭♭(A)–D; **Amaj7♭5**=A–C♯–E♭–G♯.

### *Seventh chord flat five*

C7(♭5)

Symbol: 7♭5 or 7-5

Start with a 7th chord (1–3–5–♭7) and flat the 5th.

*Examples:*

**C7♭5**=C–E–G♭–B♭. **E7♭5**=E–G♯–B♭–D. **G7♭5**=G–B–D♭–F. **B♭7♭5**=B♭–D–F♭(E)–A♭

### *Minor 7th flat five*

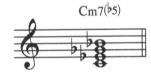

Cm7(♭5)

Symbol: min7♭5, min7-5, m7♭5, m7-5

Start with a minor 7th chord (1–♭3–5–♭7) and flat the 5th.

*Examples:*

**Cm7♭5**=C–E♭–G♭–B♭. **E♭m7-5**=E♭–G♭–B♭♭(A)–D♭. **F♯m7♭5**=F♯–A–C–E.

**Am7♭5**=A–C–E♭–G.

Please note that the minor 7th flat five chord is another name for the half-diminished 7th chord.

# Summary of Triads and Four-Note Chords

All chords can be built from the major scales found on pages 6 and 7.

Triads are three-note chords:

|  |  |
|---|---|
| Major triad | = 1–3–5 |
| Minor triad | = 1–♭3–5 |
| Diminished triad | = 1–♭3–♭5 |
| Augmented triad | = 1–3–♯5 |
| Suspended triad | = 1–4–5 |

Four-note chords are based on triads:

|  |  |  |  |
|---|---|---|---|
| Major 7th | = 1–3–5–7 | dim7 | = 1–♭3–♭5–♭♭7(6) |
| 7th | = 1–3–5–♭7 | maj7+5 | = 1–3–♯5–7 |
| 6 | = 1–3–5–6 | 7+5 | = 1–3–♯5–♭7 |
| min+7 | = 1–♭3–5–7 | 7sus4 | = 1–4–5–♭7 |
| m7 | = 1–♭3–5–♭7 | maj7♭5 | = 1–3–♭5–7 |
| m6 | = 1–♭3–5–6 | 7♭5 | = 1–3–♭5–♭7 |
| dim+7 | = 1–♭3–♭5–7 | m7♭5 | = 1–♭3–♭5–♭7 |
| ø7 | = 1–♭3–♭5–♭7 | | |

# Extended Major Scales

Any time you add notes to a scale above the first octave, those notes are called *extensions*, and the chords that use extensions are called *extended chords*. In order to build extended chords, we need to extend the major scales for a second octave. These are the same notes as the first eight notes, but an octave higher. Notice that the numbering of the scale steps continues as we extend into the second octave.

# Building Ninth Chords

Any four-note chord can be extended by adding a 9th. The 9th can be found by referring to the extended major scales on pages 12 and 13.

## Major 9th Chord

Symbol: maj9 or △9
Start with a major 7th chord and add the 9th.
*Examples:*
**Cmaj7**=C–E–G–B; add the 9th (D). **Cmaj9**=C–E–G–B–D.
**E♭maj9**=E♭–G–B♭–D–F. **Gmaj9**=G–B–D–F♯–A. **B♭maj9**=B♭–D–F–A–C.

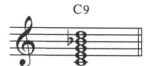

CMaj9

## Dominant 9th Chord (Usually Called a "9th Chord")

Symbol: 9
Start with a 7th chord and add the 9th
*Examples:*
**C7**=C–E–G–B♭; add the 9th (D). **C9**=C–E–G–B♭–D.
**E9**=E–G♯–B–D–F♯. **A♭9**=A♭–C–E♭–G♭ B♭. **B9**=B–D♯–F♯–A–C♯.

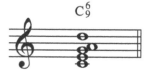

C9

## Six-Nine Chord

Symbol: 6/9
Start with a 6th chord and add the 9th.
*Examples:*
**C6**=C–E–G–A; add the 9th (D). **C6/9**=C–E–G–A–D.
**F6/9**=F–A–C–D–G. **A6/9**=A–C♯–E–F♯–B.

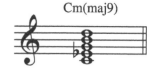

$C^6_9$

## Minor Major 9th Chord

Symbol: min maj9 or m+7+9
Start with a minor major 7th chord and add the 9th.
*Examples:*
**Cm+7**=C–E♭–G–B; add the 9th (D). **Cm+7+9**=C–E♭–G–B–D
**Dm+7+9**=D–F–A–C♯–E. **F♯m+7+9**=F♯–A–C♯–E♯(F)–G♯.

Cm(maj9)

## Minor 9th Chord

Symbol: m9 or min9
Start with a minor 7th chord and add the 9th
*Examples:*
**Cm7**=C–E♭–G–B♭; add the 9th (D). **Cm9**=C–E♭–G–B♭–D.
**Dm9**=D–F–A–C–E. **Fm9**=F–A♭–C–E♭–G. **Am9**=A–C–E–G–B.

Cm9

## Minor Six-Nine Chord

Symbol: m6/9 or min6/9
Start with a minor 6th chord and add the 9th.
*Examples:*
**Cm6**=C–E♭–G–A; add the 9th (D). **Cm6/9**=C–E♭–G–A–D.
**E♭m6/9**=E♭–G♭–B♭–C–F. **F♯m6/9**=F♯–A–C♯–D♯–G♯. **B♭m6/9**=B♭–D♭–F–G–C.

$Cm^6_9$

## Diminished 7th add 9

Symbol: dim7add9 or °7add9
Start with a diminished 7th chord and add the 9th
*Examples:*
**Cdim7**=C–E♭–G♭–A; add the 9th (D). **Cdim7add9**=C–E♭–G♭–A–D.
**Bdim7add9**=B–D–F–A♭–C♯. **Fdim7add9**=F–A♭–C♭(B)–E♭♭(D)–G.

C°7add9

## Major 9th Sharp 5

Symbol: maj9+5 or maj9♯5
Start with a major 7th chord, sharp the 5th, and add the 9th.

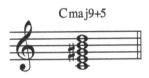

Cmaj9+5

*Examples:*
  **Cmaj7**=C–E–G–B. Sharp the G to G♯ and add the 9th (D). **Cmaj9♯5**=C–E–G♯–B–D
  **D♭maj9♯5**=D♭–F–A–C–E♭. **Emaj9+5**=E–G♯–B♯(C)–D♯–F♯. **Gmaj9♯5**=G–B–D♯–F♯–A.

## Dominant 9th Sharp 5

Symbol: 9+5 or 9♯5
Start with a dominant 7th chord; sharp the 5th and add the 9th.

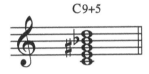

C9+5

*Examples:*
  **C7**=C–E–G–B♭; sharp the 5th (G) to G♯ and add the 9th (D). **C9♯5**=C–E–G♯–B♭–D

## 9th Chord with a Suspended 4th

Symbol: 9sus4
Start with a 7sus4 chord and add the 9th.

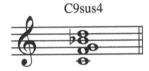

C9sus4

*Examples:*
  **C7sus4**=C–F–G–B♭; add the 9th (D). **C9sus4**=C–F–G–B♭–D

---

## Omitting Notes from 9th Chords

To make for easier fingering, it's often desirable to omit one or more notes from 9th
chords. Your first choice should be to omit the 5th of the chord unless it is sharped or flatted.
For example, the C9 chord can be played as C–E–B♭–D, leaving out the G. Your second choice is
to leave out the root. The C9 chord could be played as E–G–B♭–D.

If you have to leave out two notes, the 5th and root can both be omitted. The C9 can be played
as E–B♭–D. You'll only be using three notes but will still get the effect of a C9.

---

## Altering 9th Chords

The 5th of the chord can appear sharped, natural, or flatted.

*Examples:*
  C9♯5, C9, C9♭5

The 9th of the chord can also appear sharped, natural, or flatted.

*Examples:*
  C7♯9, C9, C7♭9

These notes can—and often do—appear in the same chord.

*Examples:*
  C7♯5♭9, C7♭5♭9, C7♯5♯9, C7♭5♯9

Since the symbols for these chords are self-explanatory they should not cause you any problems.

# Eleventh Chords

## Dominant 11th Chords (Usually Called "11th Chords")

Symbol: 11

Start with a 9th chord (1–3–5–♭7–9) and add the 11th

*Examples:*

**C11**=C–E–G–B♭–D–F; **G11**=G–B–D–F–A–C; **E11**=E–G♯–B–D–F♯–A; **A♭11**=A♭–C–E♭–G♭–B♭–D♭

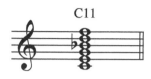

**Important note:** Unless this chord is widely spaced, it's better to omit the 3rd to avoid the harsh sound of the 3rd against the 11th. For example, in a C11, omit the E to avoid the clash against the F.

## Minor 11th Chords

Symbol: m11 or min11

Start with a minor 9th chord (1–♭3–5–♭7–9) and add the 11th.

*Examples:*

**Cm11**=C–E♭–G–B♭–D–F; **F♯m11**=F♯–A–C♯–E–G♯–B; **E♭m11**=E♭–G♭–B♭–D♭–F–A♭;

**Am11**=A–C–E–G–B–D

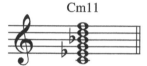

**Note:** Because the 3rd has now been lowered, the clash with the 11th no longer exists. Therefore it's perfectly all right to include both these notes.

## Augmented 11th Chords

Symbol: +11 or aug11

Start with a 9th chord (1–3–5–♭7–9) and add a sharped 11th

*Examples:*

**C+11**=C–E–G–B♭–D–F♯; **D+11**=D–F♯–A–C–E–G♯; **F+11**=F–A–C–E♭–G–B natural;

**B♭+11**=B♭–D–F–A♭–C–E natural

## Major 11th Chords

Symbol: maj11 or M11

Start with a major 9th chord (1–3–5–7–9) and add the 11th.

*Examples:*

**Cmaj11**=C–E–G–B–D–F; **Gmaj11**=G–B–D–F♯–A–C; **Emaj11**=E–G♯–B–D♯–F♯–A;

**A♭maj11**=A♭–C–E♭–G–B♭–D♭

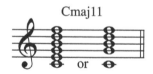

**Important note:** Unless this chord is widely spaced, it's better to omit the 3rd to avoid the harsh sound of the 3rd against the 11th. For example, in a Cmaj11, omit the E to avoid the clash against the F.

# Thirteenth Chords

## Dominant 13th Chords (Usually Called "13th Chords")
Symbol: 13
Start with an 11th chord (1–3–5–♭7–9–11) and add the 13th.
*Examples:*
**C13**=C–E–G–B♭–D–F–A; **G13**=G–B–D–F–A–C–E; **E13**=E–G♯–B–D–F♯–A–C♯;
**A♭13**=A♭–C–E♭–G♭–B♭–D♭–F

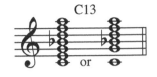

**Note:** Unless this chord is widely spaced, it's better to omit the 3rd to avoid the harsh sound of the 3rd against the 11th. For example, in a C13, omit the E to avoid the clash against the F.

## Minor 13th Chords
Symbol: m13 or min13
Start with a minor 11th chord (1–♭3–5–♭7–9–11) and add the 13th.
*Examples:*
**Cm13**=C–E♭–G–B♭–D–F–A; **F♯m13**=F♯–A–C♯–E–G♯–B–D♯; **E♭m13**=E♭–G♭–B♭–D♭–F–A♭–C;
**Am13**=A–C–E–G–B–D–F♯

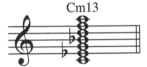

**Note:** Because the 3rd has now been lowered, the clash with the 11th no longer exists. Therefore, it's perfectly all right to include both these notes.

## 13th Chords with Augmented 11th
Symbol: 13+11 or 13aug11
Start with an 11th chord (1–3–5–♭7–9–11); sharp the 11th and add a 13th
*Examples:*
**C13aug11**=C–E–G–B♭–D–F♯–A; **D13+11**=D–F♯–A–C–E–G♯–B;
**F13+11**=F–A–C–E♭–G–B–D; **B♭13aug11**=B♭–D–F–A♭–C–E–G.

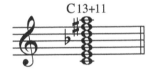

## Major 13th Chords
Symbol: maj13 or M13
Start with a major 11th chord (1–3–5–7–9–11) and add the 13th.
*Examples:*
**Cmaj13**=C–E–G–B–D–F–A; **Gmaj13**=G–B–D–F♯–A–C–E; **Emaj13**=E–G♯–B–D♯–F♯–A–C♯;
**A♭maj13**=A♭–C–E♭–G–B♭–D♭–F

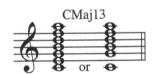

**Note:** Unless this chord is widely spaced, it's better to omit the 3rd to avoid the harsh sound of the 3rd against the 11th. For example, in a Cmaj13, omit the E to avoid the clash against the F.

## 7th add 6th chords
The 7/6 or 7add6 chord is a type of 13th chord that omits the 9th and 11th.
*Examples:*
**C7/6**=C–E–G–B♭–A; **E♭7add6**=E♭–G–B♭–D♭–C; **G♭7/6**=G♭–B♭–D♭–F♭(E)–E♭; **A7/6**=A–C♯–E–G–F♯

# More Altered Chords

The preceding pages have outlined the most common chords used in today's music. Any others you may run across will almost certainly be self-explanatory. For example, C9♭5 (sometimes written C9-5): start with a 9th chord and flat the 5th. C13♭9 (or C13-9): start with a C13 and flat the 9th.

Sometimes more than one note is altered. For example, C7♭5♭9 (or C7-5-9): start with a C7chord, flat the 5th, and add a flatted 9th. Even such seemingly difficult symbols like C13♭5♯9 (or C13-5+9) can be figured out without too much trouble.

# Omitting Notes from Extended Chords

Since extended chords like 9ths, 11ths, and 13ths have five, six, and seven notes respectively, it is often more practical to omit one or more of the notes to simplify the fingering.

### Simplifying 9th Chords
Your first choice should be to leave out the 5th. However, if the 5th is altered (sharped or flatted) leave out the root instead. This will reduce the number of notes in the chord to four, which should make it practical to play. If, however, you need to make it into a three-note chord (for example, if you're voicing it for three melody instruments) use the 3rd, 7th, and 9th. If the 5th has been altered, you can use the 3rd, 5th, and 9th or the 5th, 7th, and 9th. Personal taste also comes into play, so experiment to see which combination of sounds pleases you the most.

### Simplifying 11th Chords
Your first choice is to omit the 3rd. Next, the 5th and/or root may be omitted. If it's a minor 11th, you should keep the 3rd, as this is the note that gives the chord its minor quality. Flatted 3rd, flatted 7th, 9th, and 11th sounds good and even flatted 3rd, 9th, and 11th can be used if you must reduce the chord to three notes. Here again, don't be afraid to experiment so you can find the voicing that you think is the best.

### Simplifying 13th Chords
Always omit the 5th (unless it is altered) as your first choice. Then choose the root and the 11th as the next notes to be omitted. So, a good four-note version, of the 13th chord would be 3rd, 7th, 9th, and 13th. For a three-note version, omit the 9th.

# Voice Leading

*Voice leading* refers to how smoothly one chord moves to another. When writing for individual instruments such as human voices, woodwinds, or a brass section, voice leading is of crucial importance and overrides the choices outlined above. Singers find it easier to move stepwise or by smaller intervals than to make big skips, especially when the note they are skipping to is not in the chord they are singing. To a lesser degree, instrumentalists often have a hard time with this.

# Chords with Alternate Bass Notes

Often in today's music, you'll see a symbol such as Gm7/C or Cmaj9/A. This is a *slash chord*, which indicates that an alternate note is used as the lowest note. Sometimes, as in the above two examples, the note called for is not in the chord. Other times, as with the chords C/E or G7/B, the alternate bass note indicates which chord tone should be played as the lowest note.

# Power Chords

A *power chord* consists of the root, 5th, and octave of a major scale. The C power chord consists of the 1, 5, and 8 of the C major scale: C–G–C. The G power chord is G–D–G, and so on. It is most common to use the number 5 to refer to power chords, as in C5, G5, and E♭5. Power chords are most effective when played in the bass, as in the examples below.

Notice that the 3rd is omitted from power chords.

The first four measures of "The House of the Rising Sun" can be accompanied by these power chords in the key of E minor:

Here is another power chord sequence, this time in D minor. Notice that because power chords are missing the 3rd of the chord, they are neither major nor minor.

Rock licks sound great with power chords.

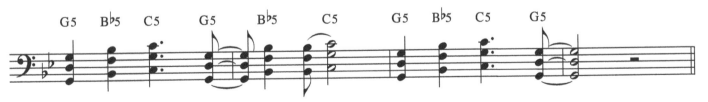

# SUMMARY

All chords can be built from the major scales found on pages 12 and 13 or from the summary on page 11.

**Triads** are three-note chords:

| | |
|---|---|
| Major | = 1–3–5 |
| Minor | = 1–♭3–5 |
| Diminished | = 1–♭3–♭5 |
| Augmented | = 1–3–♯5 |
| Suspended | = 1–4–5 |

**Four-note chords** are based on triads:

| | |
|---|---|
| Major 7th | = 1–3–5–7 |
| (dominant) 7th | = 1–3–5–♭7 |
| 6th | = 1–3–5–6 |
| min+7 | = 1–♭3–5–7 |
| m7 | = 1–♭3–5–♭7 |
| m6 | = 1–♭3–5–6 |
| dim+7 | = 1–♭3–♭5–7 |
| half-diminished 7th | = 1–♭3–♭5–♭7 |
| diminished 7th | = 1–♭3–♭5–♭♭7(6) |
| 7sus4 | = 1–4–5–♭7 |

**9th chords** are based on 7th chords:

| | |
|---|---|
| major 9th | = 1–3–5–7–9 |
| (dominant) 9th | = 1–3–5–♭7–9 |
| major 6/9 | = 1–3–5–6–9 |
| minor +7+9 | = 1–♭3–5–7–9 |
| minor 9th | = 1–♭3–5–♭7–9 |
| minor 6/9 | = 1–♭3–5–6–9 |
| 9th sus4 | = 1–4–5–♭7–9 |

**11th chords** are based on 9th chords

| | |
|---|---|
| major 11th | = 1–3–5–7–9–11 |
| (dominant) 11th | = 1–3–5–♭7–9–11 |
| augmented 11th | = 1–3–5–♭7–9–♯11 |
| minor 11th | = 1–♭3–5–♭7–9–11 |

**13th chords** are based on 11th chords

| | |
|---|---|
| major 13th | = 1–3–5–7–9–11–13 |
| (dominant) 13th | = 1–3–5–♭7–9–11–13 |
| (dominant) 13th+11 | = 1–3–5–♭7–9–♯11–13 |
| minor 13th | = 1–♭3–5–♭7–9–11–13 |

All other chords are variations on these:

| | | |
|---|---|---|
| +5 | or ♯5 | means to raise the 5th a half step |
| -5 | or ♭5 | means to lower the 5th a half step |
| +9 | or ♯9 | means to raise the 9th a half step |
| -9 | or ♭9 | means to lower the 9th a half step |
| +11 | or ♯11 | means to raise the 11th a half step |
| -13 | or ♭13 | means to lower the 13th a half step |

## Chart of Chord Tones

| Root | 3rd | 4th | 5th | 6th | 7th | 9th | 11th | 13th |
|---|---|---|---|---|---|---|---|---|
| C | E | F | G | A | B | D | F | A |
| C♯ | E♯ | F♯ | G♯ | A♯ | B♯ | D♯ | F♯ | A♯ |
| D♭ | F | G♭ | A♭ | B♭ | C | E♭ | G♭ | B♭ |
| D | F♯ | G | A | B | C♯ | E | G | B |
| E♭ | G | A♭ | B♭ | C | D | F | A♭ | C |
| E | G♯ | A | B | C♯ | D♯ | F♯ | A | C♯ |
| F | A | B♭ | C | D | E | G | B♭ | D |
| F♯ | A♯ | B | C♯ | D♯ | E♯ | G♯ | B | D♯ |
| G♭ | B♭ | C♭ | D♭ | E♭ | F | A♭ | C♭ | E♭ |
| G | B | C | D | E | F♯ | A | C | E |
| A♭ | C | D♭ | E♭ | F | G | B♭ | D♭ | F |
| A | C♯ | D | E | F♯ | G♯ | B | D | F♯ |
| B♭ | D | E♭ | F | G | A | C | E♭ | G |
| B | D♯ | E | F♯ | G♯ | A♯ | C♯ | E | G♯ |
| C♭ | E♭ | F♭ | G♭ | A♭ | B♭ | D♭ | F♭ | A♭ |

# Section 2
# Creating Chord Progressions

In this section, we discuss ways of putting chords together into progressions. You'll learn about simple two- and three-chord progressions, pedal points, how to construct progressions using diatonic and chromatic lines, what to do when a chord is repeated many times, how to put together introductions, endings and turnarounds, and how to use passing chords and neighbor chords.

## Using Roman Numerals

| Roman Numerals |
| --- |
| 1 = I |
| 2 = II |
| 3 = III |
| 4 = IV |
| 5 = V |
| 6 = VI |
| 7 = VII |

As you have learned, each note in a major scale can be thought of as a number. For example, in a C Major scale, C=1, D=2, E=3, and so on. If you think of chord progressions as numbers, you'll have no trouble playing them in any key. Customarily, Roman numerals are used for this purpose (see chart on right). In the key of C, the I chord ("the one chord") is a C major chord. The IV chord ("the four chord") is an F major chord. The V7 chord ("the five-seven chord") is a G7, and so on.

Let's say these three chords are used in a song in the key of C. You'll use the C, F, and G7 chords. But suppose you want to play the same song in the key of G. In the key of G, the I chord is G, the IV chord is C, and the V7 chord is D7, so you would use these chords to play the song. If you have trouble remembering the numbers, refer to the major scales on pages 6 and 7.

For minor chords, use a small "m." For example, IVm in the key of C is F minor. For 9th chords, use a 9; for 11th chords, use an 11; and so on. Simply substitute the Roman numeral for the letter name of the chord. If the chord is not in the scale, use a sharp or a flat. If you want an F♯ diminished chord in the key of C say: ♯IVdim ("sharp-four diminished"). If an E♭9 chord is called for (in the key of C), say ♭III9 ("flat-three ninth").

## Your First Chord Progression: I–V7–I

As you have already learned, a chord progression is when you start with a chord (usually the root chord), move to different chords, and finally return to the original root chord. The simplest form of this is I–V7–I. In the key of C, this would be C–G7–C. In the key of G, this progression would be G–D7–G. In A, it would be A–E7–A, and so on.

This simple progression can be found in many folk songs and children's songs. "Skip to My Lou" uses only the I (C) and V7 (G7) chords in the key of C.

*Skip to My Lou*

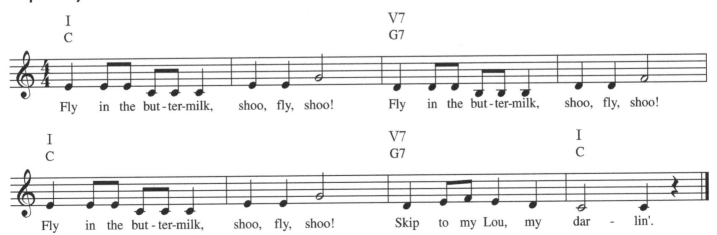

"Oh My Darling, Clementine" uses the I–V7–I (G–D7–G) progression in the key of G.

*Oh My Darling, Clementine*

## Songs That Use I–V7–I

Many other songs can be played using only the I and V7 chords in major key. Here's a partial list:

Achy Breaky Heart
Alouette
Billy Boy
Boll Weevil
Buffalo Gals
Bury Me Not on the Lone Prairie
Down in the Valley
Eency Weency Spider
Froggie Went A-Courtin'
Gentle on My Mind
Git Along Little Dogies
Go Tell Aunt Rhody
Hey Lidee
Hush Little Baby
It Ain't Gonna Rain No Mo'
La Cucaracha
Mary Ann (All Day, All Night)
Nine Men Slept in a Boarding House Bed
Old Blue
Old Chisolm Trail
Pick a Bale of Cotton
Polly Wolly Doodle
Shortnin' Bread
Simple Gifts
Streets of Loredo
Tom Dooley
Wheels on the Bus, The
Yellow Rose of Texas, The

## The I–V7–I Progression in Every Key

The most practical keys are highlighted.

C–G7–C
C♯–G♯7–C♯ (G♯7 = G♯–B♯–D♯–F♯)
D♭–A♭7–D♭
D–A7–D
E♭–B♭7–E♭
E–B7–E
F–C7–F
F♯–C♯7–F♯
G♭–D♭7–G♭
G–D7–G
A♭–E♭7–A♭
A–E7–A
B♭–F7–B♭
B–F♯7–B
C♭–G♭7–C♭

# The Im–V7–Im Progression

"Joshua Fit the Battle of Jericho" is an example of the Im–V7–Im ("one-minor, five-seven, one-minor") progression in a minor key. This arrangement is in the key of D minor. The Im chord is D minor; the V7 chord is A7. Once you're able to play the progression in D minor, try it in other minor keys (see the chart at the bottom of this page).

### Joshua Fit the Battle of Jericho

The first part of the African-American spiritual "Go Down Moses" and Hank Williams's "Ramblin' Man" also use the Im and V7 in minor keys. This progression is also used in the Jewish wedding song "Chosen Kalle Mazel Tov."

## The Im–V7–Im in All Minor Keys
(The most practical keys are highlighted.)

Cm–G7–Cm
C♯m–G♯7–C♯m
D♭m–A♭7–D♭m
Dm–A7–Dm
E♭m–B♭7–E♭m
Em–B7–Em
Fm–C7–Fm
F♯m–C♯7–F♯m
G♭m–D♭7–G♭m
Gm–D7–Gm
A♭m–E♭7–A♭m
Am–E7–Am
B♭m–F7–B♭m
Bm–F♯7–Bm
C♭m–G♭7–C♭m

# The I–♭VII–I Progression

Quite a few mountain and bluegrass tunes use the progression I–♭VII–I (say: one, flat-seven, one). In the key of G, the chords are G–F–G. Sometimes, as in the old mountain song "Little Maggie," these are the only chords used in the entire song. In other instances, this sequence is used as part of a song that also uses other chords.

In "Little Maggie," play four chords per measure.

**Little Maggie**

## Two-Chord Songs That Use Other Chords

Chase the Rising Sun—I and ♭VII
Cherry Tree Carol—I and IV
Drunken Sailor, The—Im and ♭VII
Louie, Louie—I7 and IV7
Old Joe Clark—I and ♭VII
Red Apple Juice—I and VIm
Roving Gambler, The—I and IV
Shady Grove—Im and ♭VII
Tobacco Road (Pt. 1)—Im and ♭VII

**Note:**
Legendary guitarist Bo Diddley often used only one chord, the I7, but his exciting rhythmic feel kept things interesting.

## The I–♭VII in Every Key

C–B♭
C♯–B
D♭–C♭
D–C
E♭–D♭
E–D
F–E♭
F♯–E
G♭–F♭
G–F
A♭–G♭
A–G
B♭–A♭
B–A

# Three-Chord Songs

## The I–IV–V7 Progression in a Major Key

This chord progression is one of the most useful in music. With these three chords, you can accompany hundreds, even thousands, of songs in all styles, especially folk songs, country tunes, early rock, and simple blues. In the key of C, the I, IV, and V7 chords are C, F, and G7. In the key of G, these chords are G, C, and D7. Below are a few examples.

### *Good Night Ladies*

This early blues tune uses the I–IV–V7 progression in the key of F (I=F, IV=B♭, V7=C7).

### *Careless Love*

If the above songs do not fit the singer's voice very well, experiment with changing the key. You'll find a complete list of all I–IV–V7 progressions on page 27.

"On Top of Old Smoky" is a very old folk song that makes use of the I, IV, and V7 chords in the key of C (I=C, IV=F, V7=G7). Male voices may want to transpose this song to D using D, G, and A7. Female voices may be more comfortable in G, using the G, C, and D7 chords.

### On Top of Old Smoky

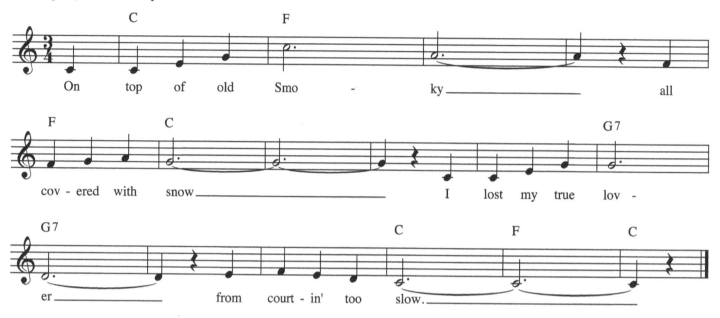

Stephen Foster's "Oh Susannah" uses the I, IV, and V7 chords in the key of D (I=D, IV=G V7=A7). Although this arrangement is in $\frac{2}{4}$ time, it will sound better if you play four chords per bar.

### Oh Susannah

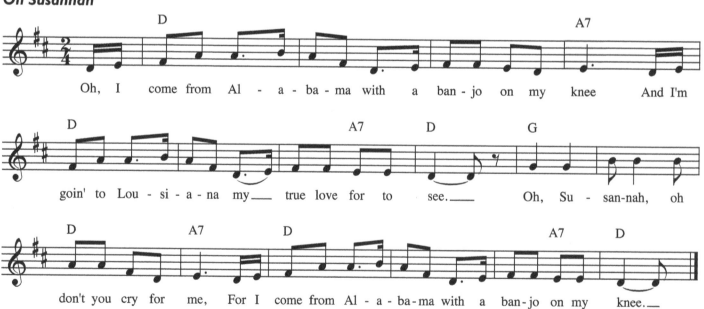

## Songs in a Major Key That Can Be Played Using Only I, IV, and V7

Act Naturally
Amazing Grace
Auld Lang Syne
Banks of the Ohio
Battle Hymn of the Republic
Beautiful Brown Eyes
Betty and Dupree
Bile That Cabbage Down
B-I-N-G-O
Black-Eyed Suzy
Blowin' in the Wind
Blue Suede Shoes
Blue-Tail Fly, The
Brahms' Lullaby
Camptown Races
Cindy
Cold, Cold Heart
Comin' Thro' the Rye
Corinna
Cotton Fields
Crawdad Song
Down by the Riverside
Erie Canal
Folsom Prison Blues
For He's a Jolly Good Fellow
Fox, The
Frankie and Johnny
Gambler, The
Gimme That Old Time Religion
Goin' Down the Road Feelin' Bad
Golden Slippers

Goodnight, Irene
Go Tell It On the Mountain
Green Green Grass of Home
Greenback Dollar
Hail! Hail! The Gang's All Here
Hand Me Down My Walkin' Cane
Hang On Sloopy
Hard, Ain't It Hard
He's Got the Whole World in His Hands
I Ride An Old Paint
I Walk the Line
If You're Happy and You Know It
Jesse James
John B. Sails
John Jacob Jingleheimer Schmit
Joy to the World (Handel)
Just a Closer Walk with Thee
Kum Ba Ya
La Bamba
L'il Liza Jane
Linstead Market
Little Brown Jug
Lolly Too Dum
Long Black Veil
Mama Don't Allow
Marines' Hymn
Matilda
Midnight Special, The
New River Train
Nine-Pound Hammer
Oh Susannah

Old Folks at Home
Old Gray Mare, The
Old MacDonald
Patsy Ory, Ory-Aye
Red River Valley
Riddle Song, The
Rock Island Line
Rock of Ages
Shall We Gather at the River
She'll be Comin' 'Round the Mountain
Silent Night
Sloop John B., The
Someone's in the Kitchen with Dinah
Sourwood Mountain
Swing Low, Sweet Chariot
There Is a Tavern in the Town
This Land Is Your Land
This Old Man
This Train
Turkey in the Straw
Twinkle, Twinkle, Little Star
Twist and Shout
Vive L'Amour
Wabash Cannonball, The
When the Saints Go Marching In
Wildwood Flower
Wimoweh (The Lion Sleeps Tonight)
Worried Man Blues
Yankee Doodle
You Are My Sunshine
Your Cheatin' Heart

## The I, IV, and V7 Chords in Every Major Key

C–F–G7
C♯–F♯–G♯7
D♭–G♭–A♭7
D–G–A7
E♭–A♭–B♭7
E–A–B7
F–B♭–C7
F♯–B–C♯7
G♭–C♭–D♭7
G–C–D7
A♭–D♭–E♭7
A–D–E7
B♭–E♭–F7
B–E–F♯7
C♭–F♭–G♭7

## The I–IV–V7 Progression in a Minor Key

In a minor key, the I and IV chords are minor, and the V7 is an ordinary 7th chord. "St. James Infirmary" is an old song about a hospital in New Orleans. This arrangement is in the key of D minor, so the Im chord is Dm, the IVm chord is Gm, and the V7 chord is A7.

### *St. James Infirmary*

I went down to the St. James In - fir-ma-ry___ To see my ba by there. She was

stretched out on a long white ta-ble___ So sweet, so cold, so fair. Let her

go, let her go, God bless her___ Where - ev-er she may be;___ She could have

searched this wide world all o - ver___ and nev-er found a sweet man like me.

## Other Songs That Use the Im, IVm, and V7 Chords

Go Down Moses (complete),
Summertime  (a simplified version)
Dark Eyes (Ochi Chornya)
Havah Nagilah
In the Pines
Raisins and Almonds
Sometimes I Feel Like a Motherless Child
Willy the Weeper

## The Im–IVm–V7 in All Minor Keys

Cm–Fm–G7
C♯m–F♯m–G♯7
D♭m–G♭m–A♭7
Dm–Gm–A7
E♭m–A♭m–B♭7
Em–Am–B7
Fm–B♭m–C7
F♯m–Bm–C♯7
G♭m–C♭m–D♭7
Gm–Cm–D7
A♭m–D♭m–E♭7
Am–Dm–E7
B♭m–E♭m–F7
Bm–Em–F♯7
C♭m–F♭m–G♭7

# Passing Chords

## Diatonic Passing Chords

A passing chord connects important chords in a progression. If the passing chords are diatonic, no accidentals are used. For example, if the basic progression is I to IV, you can use the IIm and IIIm chords as passing chords. In C this would be C to F, using Dm and Em as passing chords.

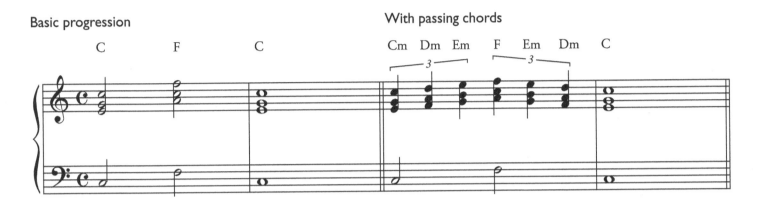

The following progression can be found in famous rock standards like "Lean On Me" and is a good example of I to IV with passing chords:

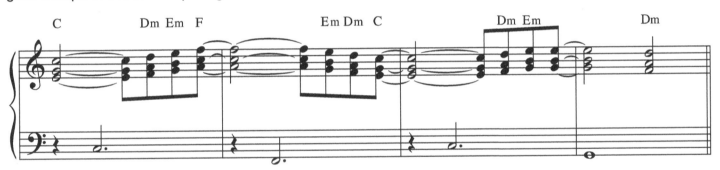

A similar idea can be used with seventh chords instead of triads. Here, the progression is Imaj7 to IVmaj7, using IIm7 and IIIm7 as passing chords. In C, this is Cmaj7 to Fmaj7, using Dm7 and Em7 as passing chords.

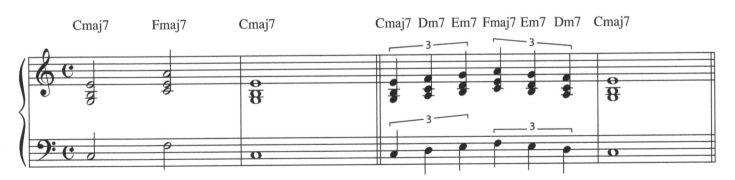

Here's a similar idea, but using five-note chords.

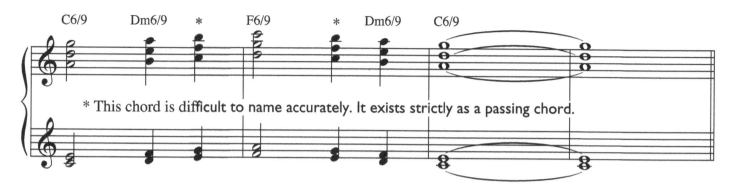

* This chord is difficult to name accurately. It exists strictly as a passing chord.

If the basic progression is VIm to IIm (as in the beginning of "Fly Me To the Moon"), you could substitute VIm7 and IIm7 as your basic chords, and V7, IVmaj7, and IIIm7 as passing chords.
In C, this would be Am7–G7–Fmaj7–Em7–Dm7.

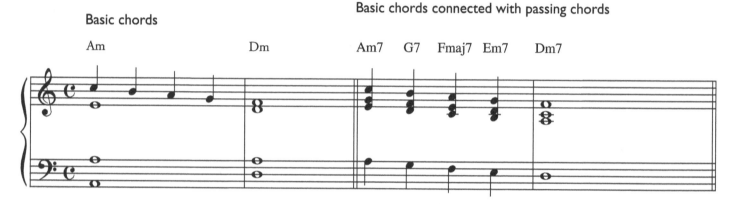

This technique works very well on a pretty tune later known as "It's All in the Game."

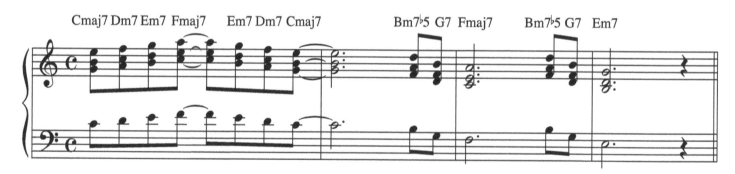

In the authors' opinions, this technique does not work as well in minor keys. However, if you wish to experiment, you can use the following chords, which are illustrated in D minor.

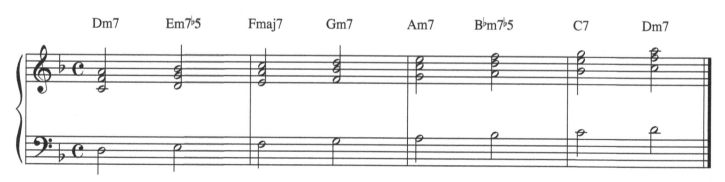

## Chromatic Passing Chords

The word "chromatic" (kro-MAT-ic) means that accidentals—notes not in the key—are used.
Chromatic passing chords are typical in jazz standards, blues, and show tunes, but rarely appear
in folk songs, country music, or rock.

Moving from I to I7 (In C: C to C7)

Basic progression:                                     With chromatic passing chords:

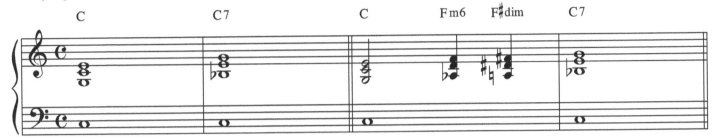

Moving from I to VI7 (C to A7). This is a typical progression used in tunes from the 1920s and
in ragtime, such as "Ja-da" or "Walk Right In."

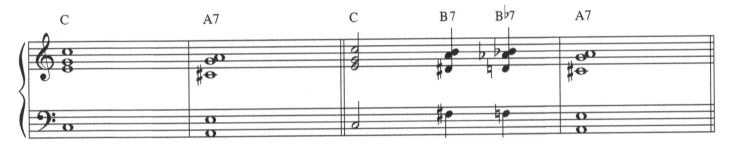

More modern versions of I to VI7.

Moving from I to IV (C to F) in more modern ways. Even though the basic progression is simple,
the passing chords add interest.

Even if you only have minimal skills at your instrument, you can experiment with connecting two
basic chords using chromatic passing chords.

## Side-Slipping

This is a special type of passing chord. It's especially easy to do on guitar because the chord shape doesn't change. The idea is simple: If two similar chords are separated by a whole step or more, you can use an in-between chord as a passing chord. In the first example below, Em7 and Dm7 are separated by a whole step. E♭m7 is a passing chord between them. In the second example (in the style of the tune "I Ain't Got Nobody," E9 and E♭9 connect F9 with D9. A simple, but effective idea.

Basic progression:                                    With side-slipping::

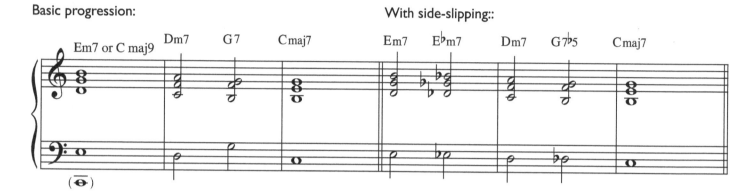

Side-slipping with 9th chords.

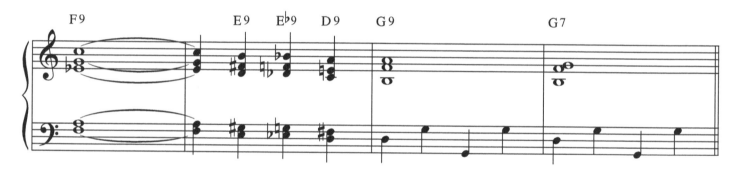

Even when chords are separated by more than a whole step (as in the example above), side-slipping can be used. Here's how you might connect the Imaj7 to the IVmaj7.

Basic progression:                                    With side-slipping:

## A Word of Caution

Because side-slipping is so easy to do—especially on guitar—some musicians have a tendency to over-use this effect. The tasteful player will limit his or her use to a few spots in a song, saving it for where it will have the most effect.

# Neighbor Chords

Basic progressions can be made more interesting by using *neighbor chords*. A neighbor chord (NC) is a chord placed before the basic chord. The NC is usually a half step above or a half step below the basic chord. For example, if the basic chord is V7, you can place a ♭VI7 or a ♯IV7 in front of it. Using a G7 as the basic chord, these would be either an A♭7 or an F♯7. Here's how you might use them in a I–V7–I progression:

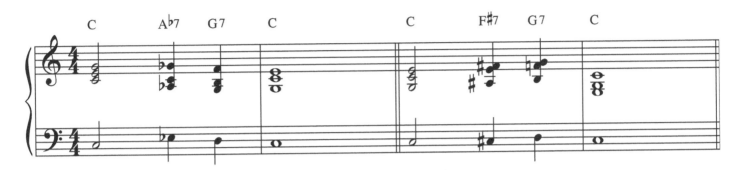

Of course, by using only triads and 7th chords, as in the above example, you'll get an old-timey sound suitable for ragtime or music from the '20s. For a more modern sound, use extensions of the chords. But remember that you're still playing the basic I–V7–I progression.

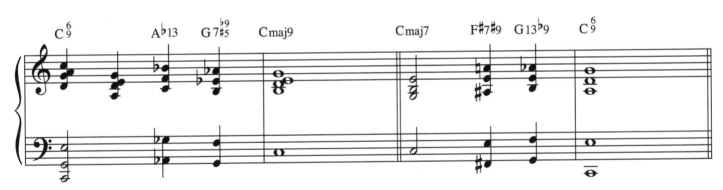

Try your own versions of the above examples. Refer to pages 92–96 for other substitutes for the I and V7 chords.

In the key of D minor, the Im–V7–Im progression (Dm–A7–Dm) might be played like this:

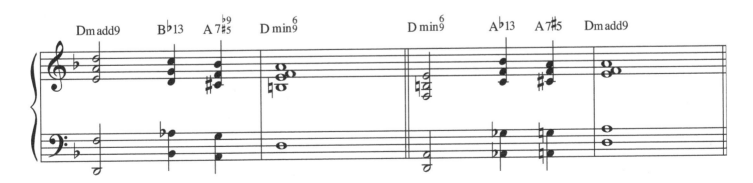

If the basic progression is I to IIIm7, you can use a IVm7 or a ♯IIm7 as the neighbor chord.

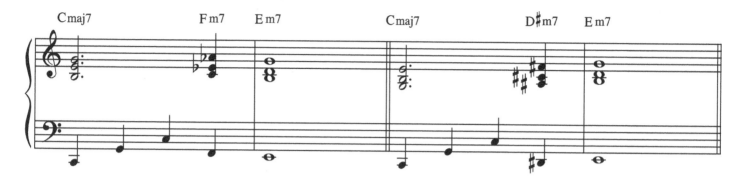

If the basic progression is I to VIm (or VI7) (C to Am or A7) ♭VII7 (B♭7) can be used as a neighbor chord.

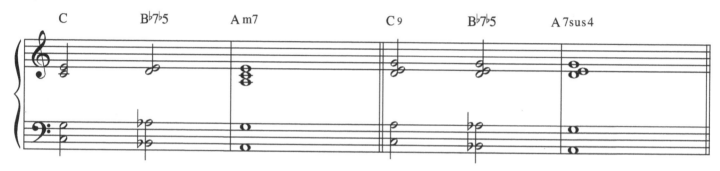

Neighbor chords can sometimes approach the basic chord from a whole step away. If the basic progression is I –V7 (C to G7) you might use the following:

Here are two ways to approach the I chord—from a whole step below and above:

By using some upper neighbor notes and some lower neighbor notes, you can create an artificial chord that really has no name. Here are four ways to approach a C6/9 chord.

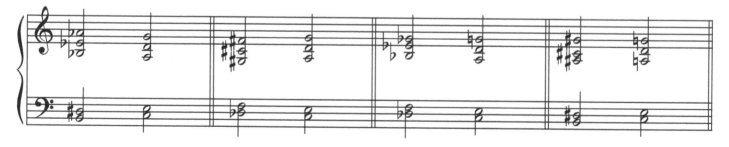

Using these techniques, you can create your own versions of neighbor chords that sound good.

# Repeated Chords

## Creating Variations

Sometimes, the same chord is repeated many times. It can very effective to just repeat it as in the Duke Ellington jazz classic, "Black and Tan Fantasy." This C Minor blues starts like this:

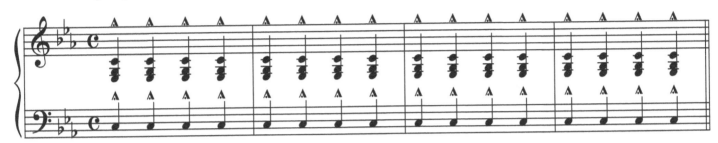

It's a simple but effective background that builds a great deal of intensity.

Billy Joel's "Keeping the Faith" and Stevie Wonder's "Superstition" (among many, many others) use an exciting rhythm to keep the interest going even though the chord doesn't often change.

A different technique is to exchange the basic chord with a neighbor chord, as in the following example in the style of The Beatles. The basic chord is I (G), but it alternates with two bars of ♭VII/I (F/G).

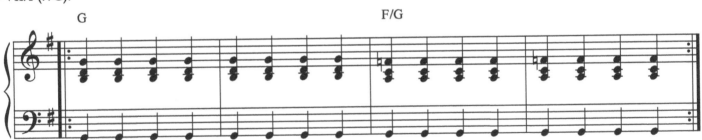

Or, you can alternate between two different versions of the I chord; for example Cmaj9 and C6.

This also works well with minor chords.

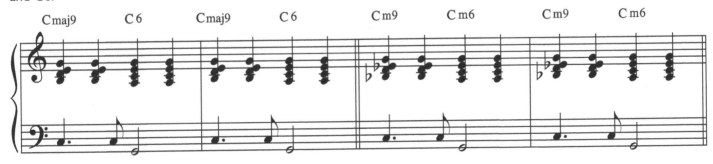

In folk or blues styles, you can add interest to a repeated I chord by alternating with the IV/I chord (alternating G and C/G in the key of G).

A variation suitable for a '50s-style rock song might be I–IV/I–I7–IV/I. In G, this would be G–C/G–G7–C/G.

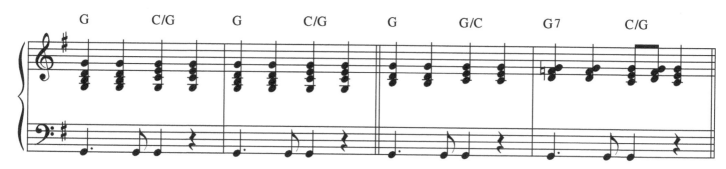

In a rock ballad, you might use an arpeggio style of accompaniment. The chord progression is still a variation on the I chord: I–IV/I–Imaj7–IV/I.

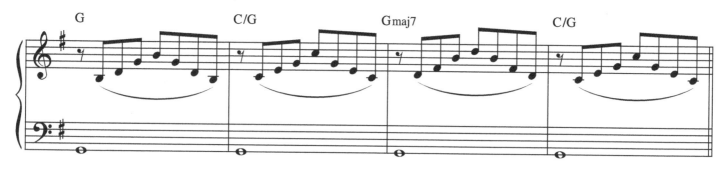

Suspending the 9th (or 2nd) of a major chord and then resolving it produces a nice ballad sound. For example, Isus2–I works nicely. In the key of C, this is Csus2–C.

This technique is also very effective in a minor key.

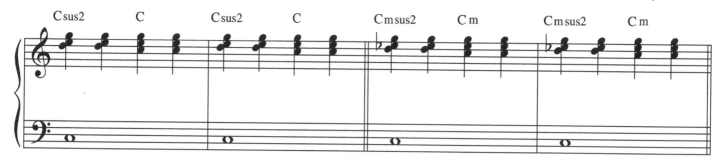

Suspending and then resolving the 4th also works well in both major and minor.

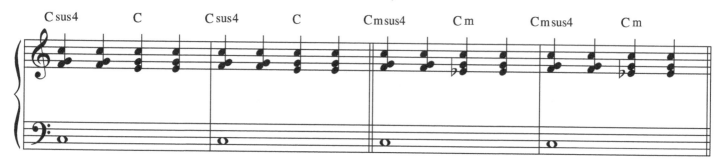

Both the 2nd and 4th may be suspended at the same time. Again, this works well in both major and minor.

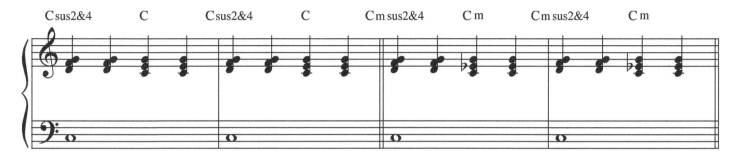

The major 7th and 6th can be added to a major chord using three-part harmony. In C, this would be Cmaj7 (C–E–G–B) and C6 (C–E–G–A). In minor, it's best to use Im7 to Im6.

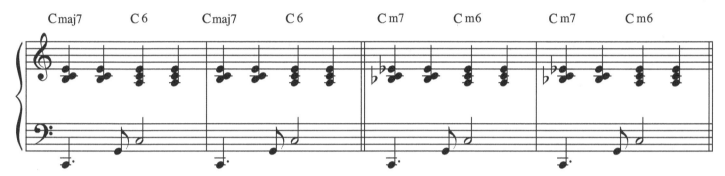

By combining all the suspended notes, you can create a line that will enhance the melody.

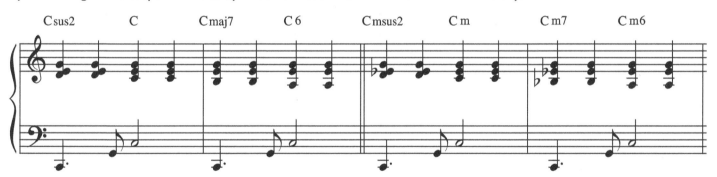

Moving the 5th of the chord by half steps creates a line like that used in the famous Glenn Miller swing-era recording of "String of Pearls" and in the Frank Sinatra recording of "In the Wee Small Hours of the Morning."

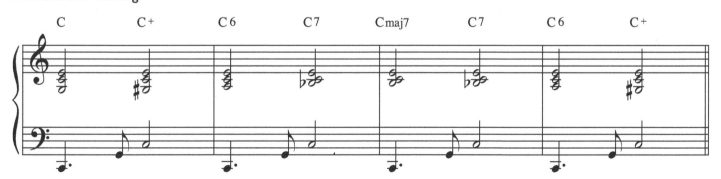

Ordinarily, C7 is not a good substitute for a C, but in this case, it acts as a passing chord from C6 to Cmaj7.

If a major chord is repeated, say, for four measures, you can create a bass line to add variety.

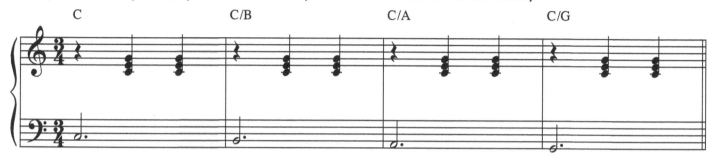

Here's a similar progression in C minor.

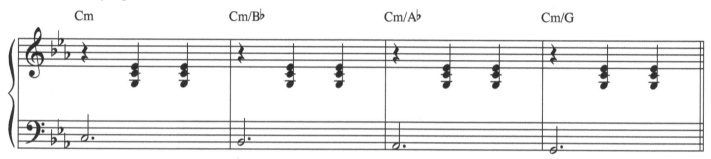

This variation on a Cm chord has been used in many tunes from the past 50 years.

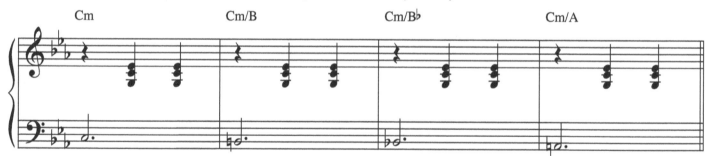

Below is nother way to create variations on a Cm chord. A similar effect is used in the James Bond theme.

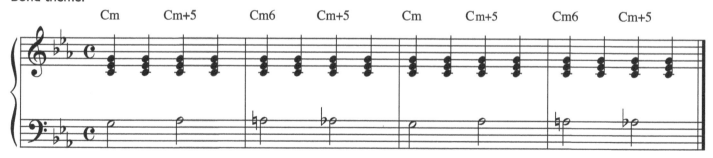

# Lines

Chord progressions can be greatly enhanced by creating *lines*, either in the bass or an inner part.
Lines are a series of notes that usually ascend or descend stepwise. The steps are most often half
steps or whole steps. Here's an example of the I to V7 progression in the key of C, using a series
of chords based on a descending chromatic line in the bass.

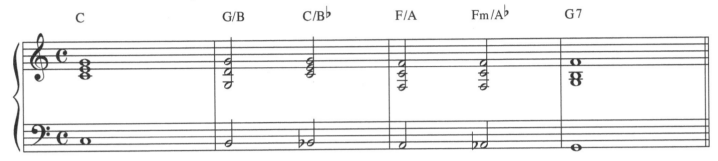

Here's one way of going from Im to IV7, using a descending line composed of whole steps:

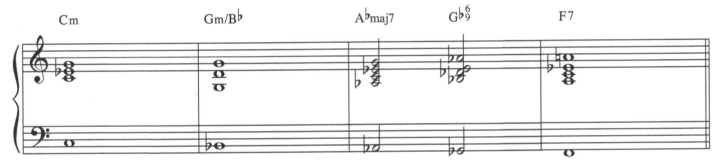

This line moves from one C chord to another, using a descending chromatic line to get there.
Notice the G pedal point (page 48) in the melody.

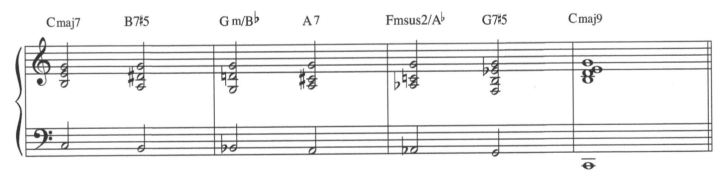

In this example, a whole-step line in the bass leads us from Cm through various chords back to
Cm. Notice that the right hand chords move up as the line moves down. This very effective device
is called *contrary motion*.

It's also effective to use lines that ascend by half steps in the bass. Many famous tunes use this effect including "Ain't Misbehavin' " and Gershwin's "Liza."

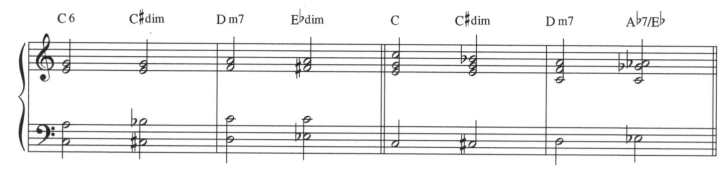

In these sequences, a rising line in the bass combines with a pedal point (see page 48) in the melody to add interest to a repeated G7 chord.

This also works backward:

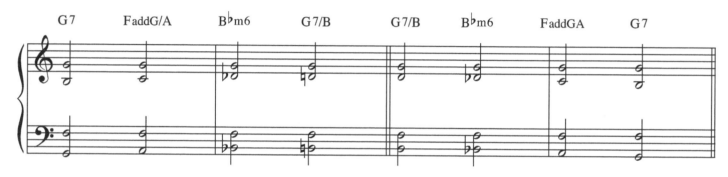

The line can also appear in an inner voice as in this example in the style of George Gershwin's jazz standard "The Man I Love." The melody is played above the following sequence:

# Turnarounds

A *turnaround* is a progression that brings a section to an end and then "turns it around" so that it leads back to the beginning. In the simplest terms, a two-bar turnaround would be I–V7 (C–G7). The ear hears the C chord as the end of the phrase. The G7 tells us that the song isn't over and that a new phrase will begin. Here are two ways to do it:

The blues demands something a little more sophisticated. Here are a few possibilities (you can also use 9ths instead of 7ths):

A ragtime-style turnaround:

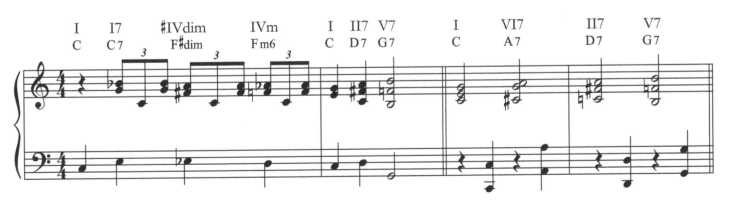

## Turnarounds from Rock Standards

In the style of Billy Joel's "Allentown," a phrase in D major ends like this: IIm/IV–I/III–Vsus4–V (Em/G–D/F♯–Asus4–A), which leads us back to the next phrase that begins on I (D major).

A standard rock 'n' roll turnaround from the 1950s is I–VIm–IV–V. Here are the basic chords in the key of C:

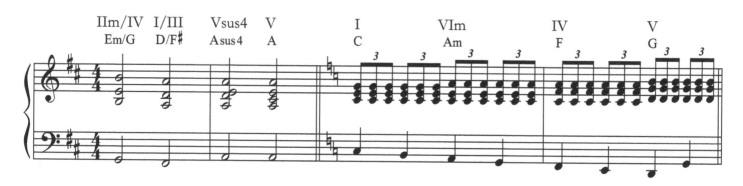

The Beatles' "Yellow Submarine" uses a simple but effective turnaround: I–VIm–IIm–IVmaj7–V. Here are the basic chords in the key of G.

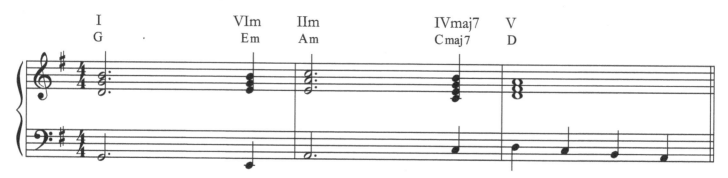

## SUMMING UP

All the above turnarounds begin with a version of the I chord and end with a V7 chord. See if you can come up with your own turnarounds.

# Endings

Almost always, when a piece comes to the final ending, the progression ends on the I chord. Several chords are usually added that bring the progression to a final conclusion. In this section, you'll find many ways of doing this. Basically, what you're doing is playing the I chord for seven beats: In the key of C, this would mean playing the C chord or a substitute for it. (For more on substitutions, see page 92).

Using the plain I chord                                          Using a 6/9 chord as a substitute

Although there are many Dixieland jazz and rock tunes that end this way, it's more usual to add some different chords to create more interest.

Using I–IV–I (C–F–C)                                          For more color use I–IVm–I (C–Fm–C)

For a more modern sound, avoid triads and use substitutes, such as suspended chords.

Using Isus2–IV6–Imaj7 (Csus2–F6–Cmaj7)                        Minor version of the same progression

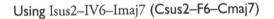

44

The ♭VII9 can substitute for IV or IVm:

Same thing using ♭VII13 instead of IV:

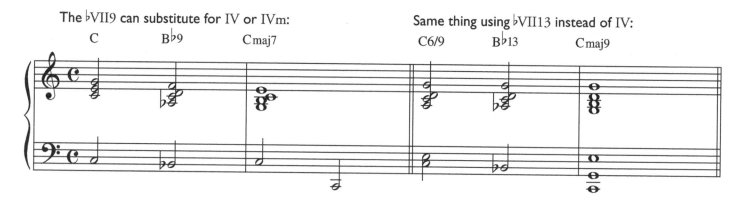

A more elaborate version of the I–IV–I progression works better at slower tempos: I–I7–IV–IVm–I. In the key of C, this becomes C–C7–F–Fm–C. This is particularly good for blues endings.

Here is the same progression with different inversions*:

Below is another version of the progression in the previous example: I–I7–IV–♯IVdim–I. In the key of C, this becomes C–C7–F–F♯dim–C.

In this version, ♭VI7 (A♭7) takes the place of ♯IVdim (F♯dim):

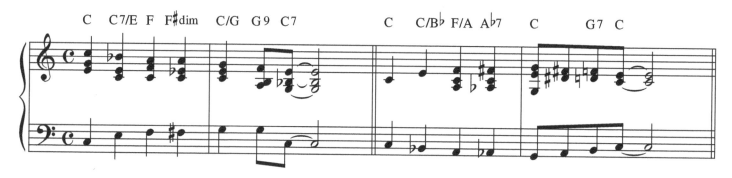

Many blues songs end with this sequence: I–I7–♯IVdim–IVm–I. In the key of C, this is: C–C7–F♯dim–Fm–C.

The IVm chord sounds even better as IVm6 (in C, Fm6).

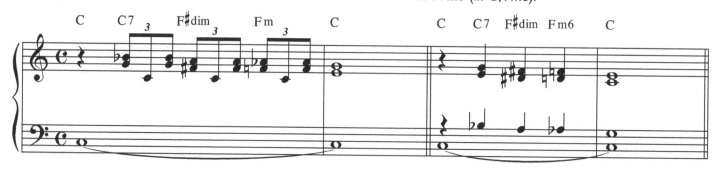

*An inversion is when the notes are in a different order. For example, a standard C chord is spelled C–E–G, but an inversion could be spelled E–G–C or G–C–E.

The second measure of the ending can also be varied. For example: I–V7–I (C–G7–C ). Using a dominant 9th chord instead of a 7th chord is typical of the blues and old-time jazz, but will sound out of place in folk songs: I–V9–I (C–G9–C). G9 is G–B–D–F–A. Even the last chord can be played as a 9th chord: I–V9–I9 (C–G9–C9). C9 is C–E–G–B♭–D. Other variations are given below.

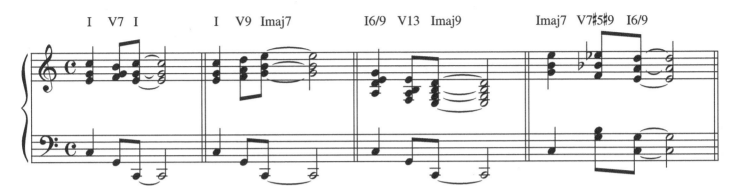

The final I chord can be approached from below.

From a half step below:                              From a whole step below:

This gospel flavored ending works well on tunes such as "Just a Closer Walk with Thee," as well as pop tunes with a gospel feel such as The Beatles' "Let It Be."

Basic progression:                                    With substitutions:

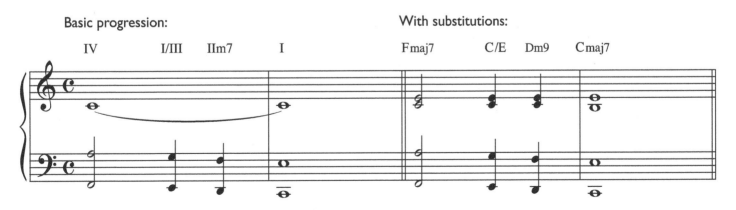

46

## False or Deceptive Endings

It can be very effective to delay getting to the I chord by inserting other chords in front of it. In
the following examples, we assume that the chord progression is heading toward a final I chord,
but we insert one or more other chords before getting there. The melody note is still a C.

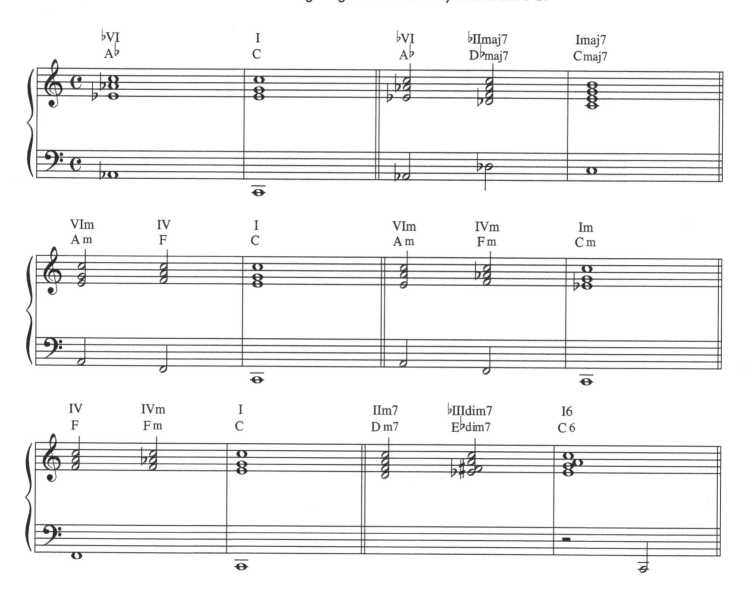

Here is a four-bar ending with a long sequence of chords that all contain the note C.

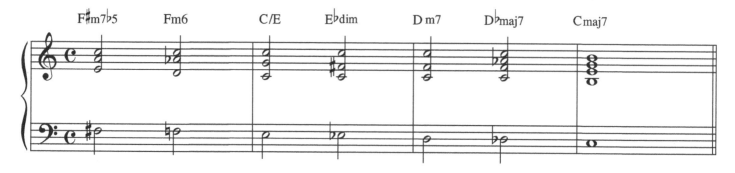

Billy Joel's "Just the Way You Are" is in the key of D. It uses a deceptive ending with a whole series of chords before finally coming to rest on the I chord. Here is a similar progression in the key of C. The progression is ♭VI–♭VII–Vm7–I7–IVm7–V7–Imaj7.

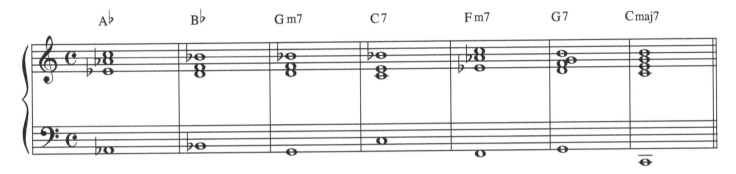

George Gershwin's great standard "Summertime" is in the key of A Minor. At the final cadence, Gershwin extends the ending with a series of chords while the soloist holds the note A.

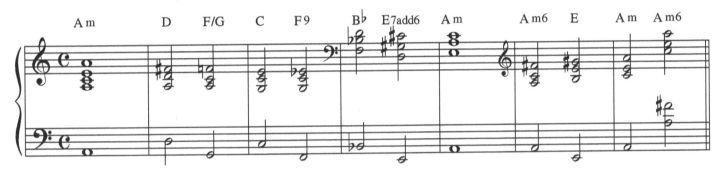

The Beatles' "Here, There and Everywhere" extends the final ending with the following sequence in the key of G: I–IIm7–IIIm–IV–I or G–Am7–Bm–C–G.

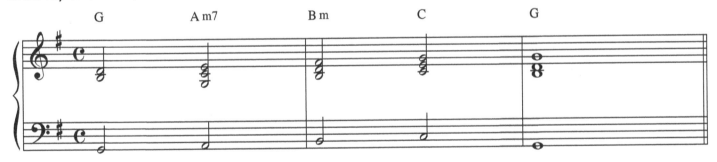

This final example is a sequence in C minor that avoids the Im chord for a few measures. Where the ear expects the Im (Cm), it gets IV7 instead. The progression then proceeds until it finally gets to Im6 (Cm6).

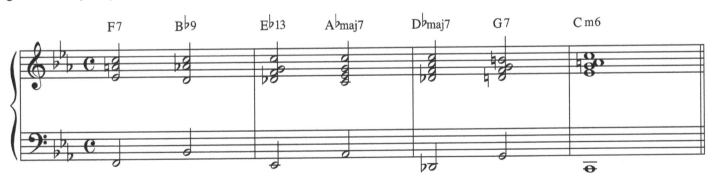

# Pedal Points

A *pedal point* is a note that is repeated or held throughout a chord sequence, even when the note does not belong to all the chords. Pedal points are usually either the root or the fifth of the scale in which the piece is written. Although the pedal point is most often found in the bass, it can occur in the top or even one of the inner voices. On the next few pages, you'll find many examples of how to use pedal points. All examples are in the key of C major or minor.

This example is I–IV/I–V7/I–I (C–F/C–G7/C–C). Although the C bass note is not part of the G7, it sounds good.

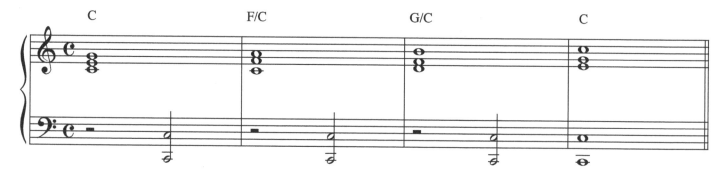

Following is a more elaborate example in C minor. The C bass note is played throughout, even when it does not fit with the chord (Dm, B♭7, G7).

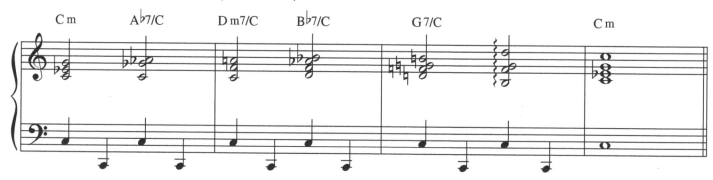

In the previous two examples, the root (C) is used in the bass. This gives a feeling of finality, so you can use it as an ending. If you wish to have a feeling of anticipation, it's better to use the 5th (G) in the bass. This next example could be used for an intro in the key of C.

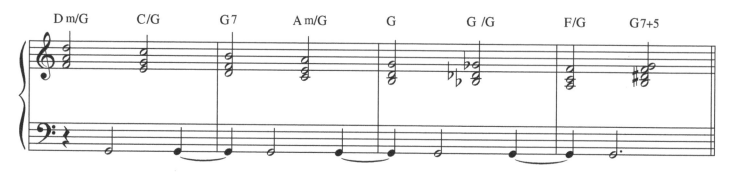

Here, the 5th is used as a pedal point in the bass in the key of C Minor.

As a general practice, it's better if the pedal point is part of the first and last chords in the progression, but this is only a suggestion, not a hard and fast rule.

The pedal point can also occur as the highest note in the progression. Here, the pedal point is the melody note (C), which is the root of the scale. Notice how the melody note becomes the 6th, 7th, major 7th, and root of the various chords.

Below, the pedal point is again the root of the scale (C), this time used with ascending progressions in major and minor.

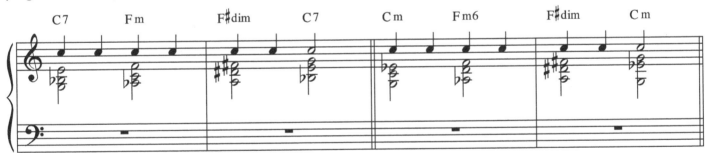

Even though the following sequence uses many chords that don't contain the C pedal point, it sounds perfectly acceptable.

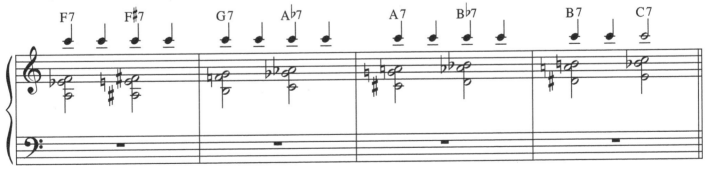

The 5th of the key (G is the 5th of C) is a very effective note to use as a melodic pedal point, as in this example in the style of the bossa nova standard "One-Note Samba." The progression is IIIm7, ♭III7, IIm11, ♭II7+11.

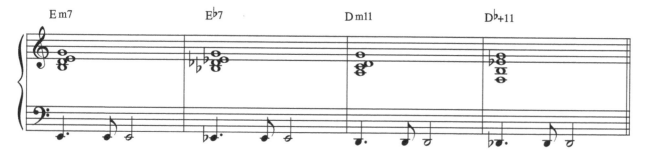

Here's a similar progression in C minor: Im, ♭III7, ♭VImaj7, ♭II+11. See the rock standard "Sunny."

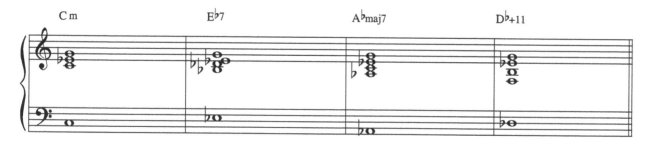

Besides the root and 5th, you can use other notes as a melodic pedal point. Here's a progression that uses the major 7th of the scale.

Here are two final examples using the 6th (A) and then the 3rd (E) of the key of C.

# Introductions

*Introductions,* or *"intros"* as most musicians call them, are played before the main part of a piece of music. Intros can consist of anything from a single chord to a sequence of two, four, or eight measures, or even longer. They serve several different purposes:

1. They indicate what the key of the music is to be; whether it is major or minor.

2. They indicate what the tempo is to be; whether it is slow, fast, or moderate.

3. They often hint at the mood of the piece; whether it is slow and sad, or fast and happy.

4. Often, they preview the song by quoting from the last four bars or from another memorable part of the tune.

In addition to the examples below, any of the progressions in the "turnaround" section can also be used as intros.

Repeat the I chord. This tells us the key and the tempo. If used with a rhythmic figure, it also suggests what kind of tune will follow.

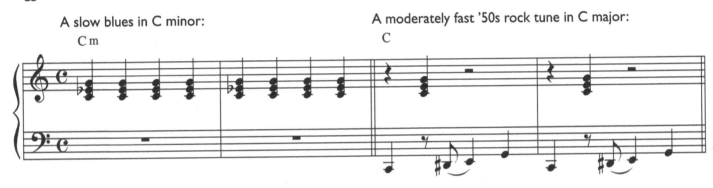

In "Good Day, Sunshine," instead of using a chord, The Beatles just play the keynote in the bass for four measures of quarter notes. Still, this tells us the key, tempo, and mood of the piece. Most intros end on the V7 chord. This tells us that something is to follow. Here's an example in the style of The Beatles' "With a Little Help from My Friends" (transposed to C from the original E major). The progression is ♭VI–V7–I–I/V–V7.

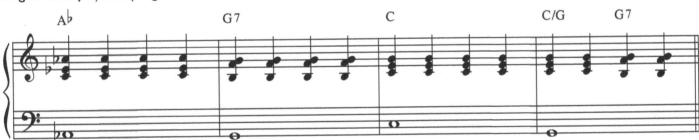

In the funk school of writing, a chord may be repeated throughout a four-bar intro. Although it's all a C chord in this example (in the style of The Jacksons' "Enjoy Yourself"), the exciting rhythm keeps the interest going.

52

Later in the same song, a highly syncopated bass line enters. This only adds to the excitement.

Played an 8va lower

Billy Joel's "Uptown Girl" uses the progression from the first four measures of the song as the intro: I–IIm–I/III–IV–V (transposed to C from the original E major). Notice the ascending diatonic line in the bass.

In "Can't Buy Me Love," a Beatles hit from 1964, the intro avoids the I chord entirely, but since all the chords are built from the C major scale, it sounds perfectly logical when the tune finally begins on the I chord. The intro consists of one measure each of IIIm–VIm–IIIm–VIm–IIm7–V.

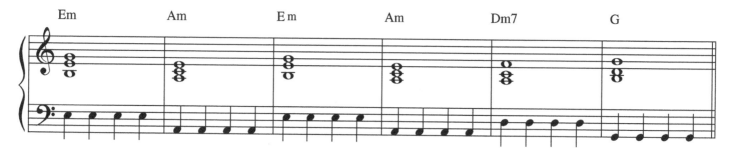

Although it's common to end intros on some form of the V or V7 chord, it's also possible to use other chords. The main thing is to create a feeling of anticipation for the music that follows. Here's an intro that can be used to introduce a progression in C minor: Im–♭III–IV–♭VI.

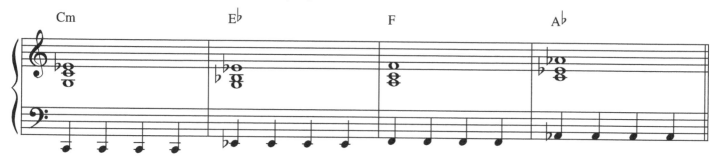

In C major, this could be I–♭III–IV–♭VI.

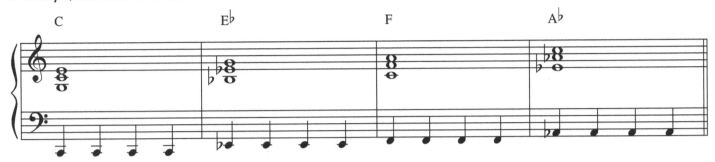

If you're going for a metal sound, try using power chords instead of triads: I5–♭III5–IV5–♭VI5.

Another possibility is to end the intro on the IV chord: I–V–♭VII–IV. This leads smoothly into C.

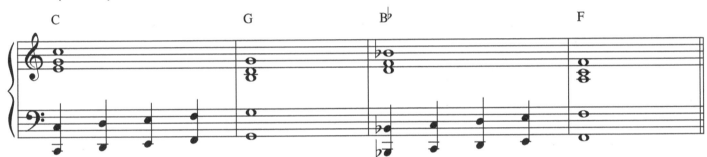

Here's a minor version of the above: Im–Vm–♭VII–IVm. This leads into C minor or major.

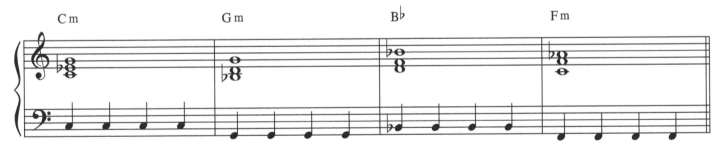

Our final example is in the style of The Beatles' "Michelle." Even though the intro ends on the V chord, it sounds as though we're headed for C minor. The C major chord comes as a pleasant surprise.

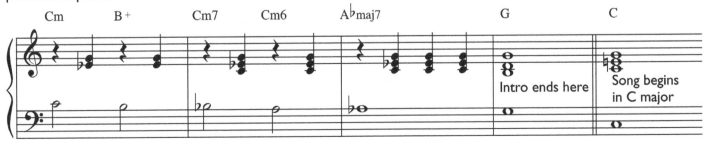

# Simplifying Chord Progressions

On the preceding pages, we discussed ways of enhancing chord progressions and making them more interesting by adding pedal points, creating lines, and using passing and neighbor chords. Sometimes, however, it's useful to know how to simplify existing chord progressions that use all of these devices. There are several possible reasons for doing this.

1. If you're just starting out on a chordal instrument such as keyboard, guitar, or banjo, you may want to simplify existing chord progressions in order to adapt the music to your level of skill. Just leave out all the devices that you've learned in this book and restore the progression to its basics. For example, if you see a 6th, major 7th, 6/9, or major 9th, just play a major triad. A minor 6th, minor 7th, minor/major 7th, or minor 9th can be played as a plain minor triad. Any extended or altered forms of the 7th chord, diminished, or augmented chords can be simplified back to the basic 7th chord, or even a triad. For example, the first 12 measures of Jerry Herman's "I Don't Want to Know" use the I, I6, and Imaj7. These can all be played as a I chord. The 7th and 8th measures of Vincent Youmans' "Time on My Hands" uses these substitutes for a C7 chord: C7–C9–Gm7/C–C7. Simplify this to eight beats of C7.

2. Or, you might want to simplify the key. For example, the great standard "Stardust" is written in the key of D♭ (five flats). The first three chords of the chorus are G♭–G♭m–D♭ (IV–IVm–I). Since D♭ is a fairly difficult key, it would simplify things greatly to transpose the chord progression to the key of C (no sharps or flats). Now, the first three chords would be F–Fm–C. To transpose a progression to another key:

   Step 1: Label the existing chords with Roman numerals.
   Step 2: Choose a simpler key.
   Step 3: Write in the letter names of the chords in the new key (or do this mentally if you can).

3. Similar to the above, if you're a soprano or a tenor, you can probably sing most sheet music in the key in which it's written. If you're an alto or a baritone, you'll sometimes want to sing in a lower key. You can use the technique described above to do this. For example, "Climb Every Mountain" (from *The Sound of Music*) is written in the key of C. The lowest note is C; the highest note is F. If you're a soprano or tenor you'll probably find this key to be satisfactory. But if you're an alto or baritone, it will probably be too high. A key that's lower would be B♭ (low note B♭, high note E♭). If you're a high soprano or tenor, you might even prefer a higher key such as D (low note D, high note G).

4. Another reason for simplifying chord progressions is to facilitate improvisations. If your style of improvising is to "run the changes," it may sound fussy and stilted to attempt using every passing chord and substitution. A better plan is to reduce the progression to its basics and use that as the basis for your improvisations.

# SECTION 3
# CHORD PROGRESSIONS IN DIFFERENT STYLES

In this section, we illustrate chord progressions from the last 100 years of American music. We'll look at everything from blues, folk, and ragtime to the latest progressions from the first decades of the 21st century.

## Blues Chord Progressions

Blues music involves a re-thinking of the major scale. For example, the C major scale contains the notes C–D–E–F–G–A–B–C. In the blues scale, both the 3rd and the 7th are lowered a half step. Sometimes the 5th is lowered a half step as well. The C blues scale consists of the notes C–D–Eb–F–G (or Gb)–A–Bb–C. The way blues guitarists do it, blue notes, especially the 3rd, are often "bent" (raised in pitch by pushing the string across the fingerboard) so that the resulting note is somewhere between E flat and E natural, the so-called "neutral 3rd." Since this is impossible on keyboard unless you have a "pitch bend" attachment, pianists often compensate by playing quick repeated slurs, which include the flatted and natural 3rd.

Because of the use of flatted scale tones in the blues, the I7 chord (which includes Bb, the flatted 7th) often replaces the I and the IV7 chord (which includes the Eb, the flatted 3rd) often replaces the IV chord.

### The 12-Bar and 8-Bar Blues

The most basic form of the blues is the *12-bar blues*. It's played in 4/4 time with the following progression:

```
I / / /   | I / / /   | I / / /   | I7 / / /
IV / / / | IV / / / | I / / /   | I / / /
V7 / / / | V7 / / / | I / IV / | I / V7 /
```

> A slash / represents one beat. A Roman numeral followed by three slashes represents four beats.

**In C** this would use the C, C7, F, and G7 chords.
**In G** the chords would be G, G7, C, and D7.
**In F** the chords would be F, F7, Bb, and C7.
**In Bb** the chords would be Bb. Bb7. Eb, and F7.
**In D** the chords would be D, D7, G, and A7.

The last two measures are called a turnaround. These chords complete the progression and lead the way to the next *chorus* (repetition of the form). See the "Turnarounds" and "Endings" sections on pages 41–47 for more on this important technique.

---

*Variation I—Adding More 7th Chords*

```
I / / /   | I / / /   | I / / /   | I7 / / /
IV7 / / / | IV7 / / / | I / / /   | I7 / / /
V7 / / /  | V7 / / /  | I I7 IV7 /| I / V7 /
```

**In C** use the C, C7, F7, and G7 chords.
**In G:** G, G7, C7, and D7.
**In F:** F, F7, Bb7, and C7.
**In Bb:** Bb. Bb7. Eb7, and F7.
**In D:** D, D7, G7, and A7.

### Variation 2—Substituting the IV7 for the I or the V7

```
I / / /   | IV7 / / / | I / / /  | I7 / / /
IV7 / / / | IV7 / / / | I / / /  | I / / /
V7 / / /  | IV7 / / / | I / IV7 / | I / V7 /
```

This variation uses the same chords as Variation 1.

### Variation 3—Getting More Motion Into the 12-Bar Blues Progression

This variation gets a more sophisticated sound by changing chords every two beats. In addition to the usual blues chords, major- and minor-6th chords are utilized.

```
I / I7 /        | IV / IVm /   | I / I6 /  | I / I7 /
IV / IV6 /      | IVm / IVm6 / | I / I6 /  | I7 / I6 /
♭VI7 / V7 /     | ♭VI7 / V7 /  | I / IV /  | I / V7 /
```

In addition to the chords you've been using, this version uses IVm, I6, IV6, IVm6, and ♭VI7 chords:

**In C:** Fm, C6, F6, Fm6, and A♭7
**In G:** Cm, G6, C6, Cm6, and E♭7
**In F:** B♭m, F6, Fm6, and D♭7
**In B♭:** E♭m, B♭6, B♭m6, G♭7
**In D:** Gm, D6, G6, Gm6, and B♭7

### Variation 4—Using the ♯IV Diminished Chord

This chord can substitute for a IV or IVm when leading back to the I chord.

```
I / I7 /     | IV / ♯IVdim / | I / I6 / | I / I7 /
IV / IV6 /   | ♯IVdim / / /  | I / I6 / | I7 / I6 /
♭VI7 / V7 /  | ♭VI7 / V7 /   | I / IV / | I / V7 /
```

In addition to the chords used in Variation 3, the ♯IVdim is used. Please note that this chord is actually a diminished 7th; the 7 is taken for granted.

**In C:** F♯dim (F♯–A–C–E♭)
**In G:** C♯dim (C♯–E–G–B♭)
**In F:** Bdim (B–D–F–A♭)
**In B♭:** Edim (E–G–B♭–D♭)
**In D:** G♯dim (G♯–B–D–F)

All the above chord progressions are variations on the 12-bar blues. However, not all blues forms use this structure. Some have 16 bars.

### Variation 5—"Frankie and Johnny"

This very old blues tune started out as "Frankie and Albert" in the 1880s or 1890s. It's based on an actual murder case that took place around that time. Notice that the IV chord is held for two extra beats. The ♯IVdim is a passing chord that leads back to the I chord. The ♭VI7 is a neighbor chord to the V7 that follows it.

```
I / / /   |I/ / / |I/ / /           |I7 / / /
IV / / / |IV/ / / |IV / ♯IVdim /  |I / / ♭VI7
|V7 / / / |V7 / / / |I / IV7 /       |I / V7 /
```

This blues is usually played in the key of C where the chords would be:

```
C / / /   |C/ / / |C/ / /           |C7 / / /
F / / /   |F/ / / |F / F♯dim /   |C / / A♭7
G7 / / / |G7 / / / |C / F7 /       |C / G7 /
```

### Variation 6—"How Long Blues"

Leroy Carr wrote this great standard in 1929. It consists of an eight-bar phrase.

```
I / / / |I7 / / / |IV / / /|IVm / / /
I / / / |V7 / / / |I  I7 ♯IVdim VIIdim |I / V7 /
```

In the key of C, this would be:

```
C / / / |C7 / / / |F / / /             |Fm / / /
C / / / |G7 / / / |C C7 F♯dim Bdim |C / G7 /
```

### Variation 7—"Trouble in Mind"

Another great blues standard, this one was written by Richard M. Jones in 1926. It also uses an eight-bar progression:

```
I / / / |V7 / / / |I7 / / / |IV / / /
I / / / |V7 / / / |I / IV / |I / V7 /
```

In the key of G, this would be:

```
G / / / |D7 / / / |G7 / / / |C / / /
G / / / |D7 / / / |G / C / |G / D7 /
```

### Variation 8—"Key to the Highway"

One of Big Bill Broonzy's most famous compositions, "Key to the Highway" is still another variation on the eight-bar blues.

```
I / / / |V7 / / / |IV / / / |IV / / /
I / / / |V7 / / / |I / / /    |V7 / / /
```

In the key of F, this would be:

```
F / / / |C7 / / / |B♭ / / / |B♭ / / /
F / / / |C7 / / / |F / / /    |C7 / / /
```

58

### Variation 9—"Jailhouse Blues"

Clarence Williams and the immortal Bessie Smith collaborated on this sophisticated 12-bar blues in 1923. The V7+ chord is a variation on the V7 chord. The ♭VI7 is a neighbor chord to the V7.

```
I / / /   |V7+ / / /  |I / / /|I7 / / /
IV7 / / /|♭VI7 / V7 /|I / / /|I / / /
V7 / / /  |♭VI7 / V7 /|I / / /|I / V7 /
```

In the key of F, this would be as shown below. Note that the V7+ chord is C7aug (C–E–G♯–B♭) and the ♭VI7 chord is D♭7 (D♭–F–A♭–C♭ or B).

```
F / / /    |C7aug / / /|F / / /|F7 / / /
B♭7 / / /  |D♭7 / C7 / |F / / /|F / / /
C7 / / /   |D♭7 / C7 / |F / / /|F / C7 /
```

### Variation 10—Leadbelly Variation

Huddie Ledbetter, better known as Leadbelly, was discovered in prison where he was serving a term for murder. His singing and 12-string guitar playing so impressed the governor of the state that he pardoned Leadbelly and the singer guitarist went on to a successful career.

Leadbelly was fond of starting blues forms on the I7 chord. Some of these tunes used only the I7 and the ♭VII chords. In the key of A, this would be A7 and G. The key center in these songs is ambiguous. "The Mamas and the Papas" used this progression as the basis for their hit song "Creeque Alley."

### Variation 11—Ragging the Blues

In the Carolinas, Virginia, and Georgia, many blues players were influenced by ragtime chord progressions. One of the most popular of these progressions is I –VI7–II7–V7–I. Blind Boy Fuller, a guitarist and songwriter fron North Carolina, has recorded dozens of songs that use this progression.

In the key of C, this would be

```
C / / /|A7 / / /|D7 / / /|G7 / / /|C / / /
```

The tune "Walk Right In" uses the progression this way:

```
C / / /   |C / A7 /|D7 / G7 /|C / / /
C / / /   |C / A7 /|D7 / / / |G7 / / /
C7 / / /|C7 / / / |F7 / / /  |F7 / / /
C / / /   |C / A7 /|D7 / G7 /|C / / /
```

### Variation 12—Another Ragtime Progression

This progression starts out like the first eight measures of a standard 12-bar blues...

```
I / / /   |I / / /  |I / / /  |I7 / / /
IV / / / |IV7 / / / |I / / /  |I7 / / /
```

...but then continues like this:

```
IV / I / | II7 / V7 / | I / IV / | I / V7 /
```

In C, this would be:

```
C / / / |C / / /   |C / / / |C7 / / /
F / / / |F7 / / /  |C / / / |C7 / / /
F / C / |D7 / G7 / |C / F / |C / G7 /
```

## Country Blues

Country blues tends to be more abstract than the blues performed by most contemporary players. A typical blues song uses the following lyrics structure (example from W. C. Handy's "St. Louis Blues"):

Line 1— I hate to see that evening sun go down,

Line 2—I hate to see that evening sun go down, (repeat of Line 1 with a similar melody but different chords)

Line 3—'cause my baby, he (she) done left this town. (A sort of answer line to what has been presented so far.)

### Blind Lemon Jefferson

In country blues, sometimes the second line is repeated instead of the first. Here's a 16-bar blues chord progression used by the great country blues singer Blind Lemon Jefferson:

```
I / / /  |I / / /  |I / / /  |I7 / / /
V / / / |V / / / |V / / / |V / / /
V / / / |V / / / |V / / / |V / / /
V / / / |IV / / / |I / / / |I / / /
```

In the key of C, this would be:

```
C / / / |C / / / |C / / / |C7 / / /
G / / / |G / / / |G / / / |G / / /
G / / / |G / / / |G / / / |G / / /
G / / / |F / / / |C / / / |C / / /
```

### Another 16-Bar Blues Progression

```
I / / /    | I / / /      | I / / /   | I7 / / /
IV / / /   | IV / / /     | I / / /   | I / / /
V / / /    | V / / /      | IV / / /  | IV / / /
I / I7 /   | IV / #IVdim / | I / IV /  | I / V7 /
```

In G, this would be:

```
G / / /        | G / / /        | G / / /        | G7 / / /
C or C7 / / /   | C or C7 / / /  | G / / /        | G / / /
D / / /         | D / / /        | C or C7 / / /  | C or C7 / / /
G / G7 /        | C / C#dim /    | G / C /        | G / D7 /
```

Other variations include playing line 3 as…

```
D7 / / / | C7 / / / | D7 / / / | C7 / / /
```

…or starting Line 1 with a 7th chord:

```
G7 / / / | C7 / / / | G / / / | G7 / / /
```

## Minor Blues

Some blues singers prefer using minor chord progressions.

### Walter Davis

Walter Davis, a piano player from Cincinnati, was one blues singer who liked to use minor chords in his songs. Here's an example of a 12-bar blues in minor key:

```
Im / / /   | Im / / /    | Im / / /  | Im7 / / /
IVm / / /  | IVm7 / / /  | Im / / /  | Im7 / / /
Vm / / /   | IVm / / /   | Im / IVm / | Im / Vm7 /
```

In the key of A minor, this would be:

```
Am / / /   | Am / / /    | Am / / /  | Am7 / / /
Dm / / /   | Dm7 / / /   | Am / / /  | Am7 / / /
Em / / /   | Dm / / /    | Am / Dm / | Am / Em7 /
```

### Curtis Jones

Curtis Jones's "Highway 51 Blues" uses this interesting minor progression. Notice the mixing of the minor I chord (Am) with the IV7 (D7) and V7 (E7) chords from the major.

```
Am / / / | D7 / / / | Am / / / | A7 / / /
D7 / / / | D7 / / / | Am / / / | A7 / / /
D7 / / / | D7 / / / | Am / / / | E7 / / /
```

### Mixing Major and Minor

Another variation uses the I and IV chords in minor with the V7 from the major:

```
Am / / / | Dm / / / | Am / / /    | A7 / / /
Dm / / / | Dm / / / | Am / / /    | Am / / /
E7 / / /  | E7 / / /  | Am / Dm / | Am / E7 /
```

### Changing Chords Every Two Beats

Yet another variation keeps the motion going by changing chords every two beats:

```
Am / Dm / | Am / Dm / | Am / Dm / | Am / Dm /
Dm / G7 / | Dm / G7 / | Am / Dm / | Am / Dm /
F7 / E7 /  | F7 / E7 /  | Am / Dm / | Am / E7 /
```

### The "Barbershop Chord"

The ♭VI7 chord is nicknamed "The Barbershop Chord" because of its use in an 1890–1910 type of unaccompanied vocal harmony called, appropriately enough, "barbershop harmony." It's often heard in many types of music. The late romantic period composers like Brahms and Tchaikovsky were fond of it, and many pop songs included it through the years. You can use it to good effect in the blues to substitute for the I chord in the second measure of the progression and as a neighbor chord played before the V7 chord in the turnaround. For example:

```
I / / /    | ♭VI7 / / / | I / / / | I7 / / /
IV / / /  | IV7 / / /   | I / / / | VI7 / / /
II7 / / / | V7 / / /    | I / / / | ♭VI7 / V7 /
```

In the key of C, this would be:

```
C / / /    | A♭7 / / / | C / / / | C7 / / /
F / / /    | F7 / / /   | C / / / | A7 / / /
D7 / / / | G7 / / /   | C / / / | A♭7 / G7 /
```

This works very well in minor blues also:

```
Im / / /   | ♭VI7 / / /  | Im / / / | I7 / / /
IVm / / / | IVm7 / / / | Im / / / | VI7 / / /
II7 / / /  | V7 / / /     | Im / / / | ♭VI7 / V7 /
```

In the key of C minor, this would be:

```
Cm / / / | A♭7 / / / | Cm / / / | C7 / / /
Fm / / / | Fm7 / / / | Cm / / / | A7 / / /
D7 / / / | G7 / / /   | Cm / / / | A♭7 / G7 /
```

> ### Swamp Blues
>
> The late, great blues singer and composer, Muddy Waters, liked to use this chord progression in some of his tunes: I–♭III–IV. This relatively simple chord modification produces a characteristic Delta blues sound that is unlike any of the progressions we have discussed. In D, this would be:
>
> ```
> D / F G  | D / F G  | D / F G | D / F G
> G / B♭ C | G / B♭ C | D / F G | D / F G
> A / C D  | G / B♭ C | D / F G | D / F G
> ```
>
> This is very similar to the rock standard "Green Onions."

## Swing, Boogie-Woogie, and Bebop Blues

During the era of big band swing, about 1932–1950, many hit songs were written based on the blues. Woody Herman even called his band (1936–1946) "The band that plays the blues." His first big hit was "Woodchopper's Ball" (1939), which was a 12-bar blues. The only concession to modernism was the use of 6ths and 9ths. Here's the chord progression in the recorded key of C (notice that no turnaround is used):

Although boogie-woogie had been known and played since the 1920s, it wasn't until about 1940 that it became a national and international craze. An example of a song from this period is "The Boogie-Woogie Bugle Boy of Company B," as recorded by The Andrews Sisters. The progression was a 12-bar blues, but the difference was the bass line, which was played "eight to the bar." Here's the progression to "Boogie-Woogie Bugle Boy" transposed to C:

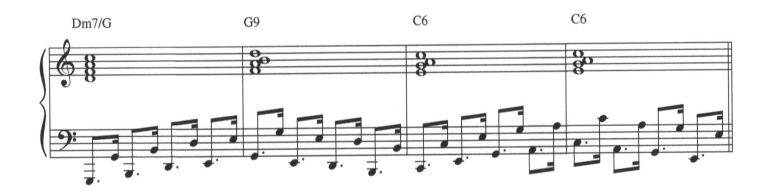

Bebop first appeared in the early 1940s in the playing of Thelonious Monk, Kenny Clarke, Charlie Christian, and especially those two giants of music, Charlie Parker and Dizzy Gillespie. Parker was fond of the blues, and by using tonicization (see page 95) and many extended and altered chords, he took the blues progression to places undreamed of by traditional blues players. Here's the 12-bar blues progression to "Bloomdido":

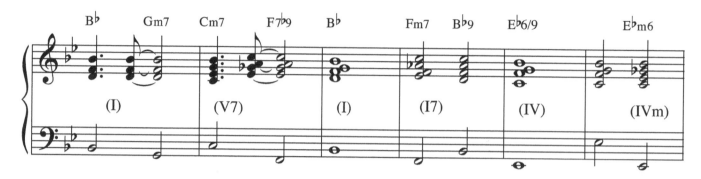

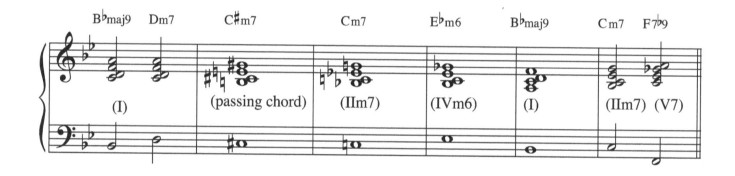

# Early Rock

## Blues in Early Rock

Early rock was heavily influenced by rhythm and blues (R&B), and many of the hits from the 1950s and early '60s were based completely or in part on the 12-bar blues progression. Usually measures 9 and 10 used the V7 and IV7 chords as in the following example.

Here's a partial list of rock and country rock tunes that use this progression:

Good Golly, Miss Molly
Long Tall Sally
I Almost Lost My Mind
What'd I Say
Peppermint Twist
Charlie Brown
Dizzy Miss Lizzie
At the Hop
Hound Dog
Ready Teddy
Johnny B. Goode

Other tunes make a few changes, but keep the 12-bar pattern intact:

Don't Be Cruel (IIm7 in meas. 9, V7 in meas. 10)
C.C. Rider (V7 continues through meas. 9 and 10)
Since I Met You Baby (IV substitutes for I in meas. 2)
Shake, Rattle and Roll (IIm7 in meas. 9; V7 in meas. 10)
Maybellene (like C.C. Rider)
Rock Around the Clock (chorus only, like Shake, Rattle and Roll

Here are a few examples of early rock tunes based on a 16-bar blues. The I chord is extended for eight measures, but then the blues continues as usual.

Rockin' Robin
Blue Suede Shoes
Jailhouse Rock

## The I–VIm–IIm–V7 Progression

Although the I–VIm–IIm–V7 progression had been used long before the 1950s, as in George
Gershwin's "I Got Rhythm" (1930), it was only in the '50s that the progression came into its own.
In the rock and roll of that period, the I was usually a triad, the VI and II chords were either
minor triads or minor 7ths, and the V chord was either a triad or a 7th chord.

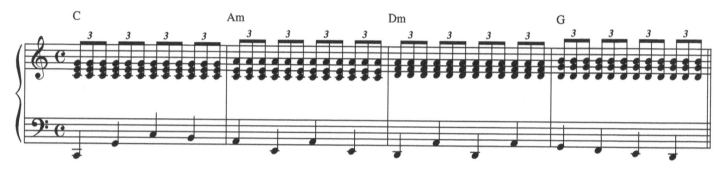

Here's the same progression using minor 7ths and the V7 chord:

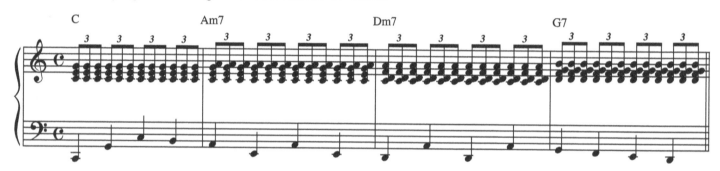

Sometimes, the third measure is played as a IV chord:

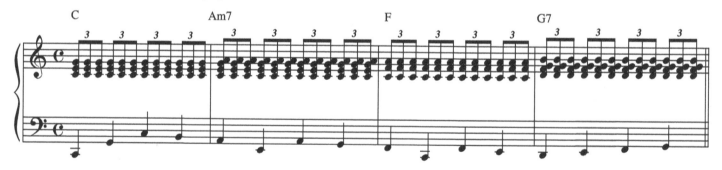

Many hit songs were based on this progression. Here are a few of them:

Why Do Fools Fall in Love
Stand By Me
Sh-Boom
There Goes My Baby
Come and Go with Me (Pt. 1)
Book of Love
Diana
Duke of Earl
Earth Angel
Lollipop
A Teenager in Love

## The I, IV, and V Chords in Early Rock

Many early rock songs were written using the I, IV(7), and V(7) chords, the same chords as used in the blues, but appearing in different orders. Here are some examples of different ways these chords were used.

### Great Balls of Fire

Two measures of I, two measures of IV7, one measure each of V7 and IV7 followed by two measures of I.

### Spanish Harlem

Eight measures of I, five measures of IV, two measures of I, four measures of V, and four measures of I.

### All Shook Up

Eight measures of I, one measure each of IV7 and V7, two measures of I. This phrase is repeated, and is followed by a bridge consisting of two measures each of IV7, I, IV7, and V7. The opening phrase then repeats.

### Rock and Roll Music

Chuck Berry's "Rock and Roll Music" starts out like a blues but goes in some other directions: Three measures of I, one measure of I7, two measures of IV7, two measures of I, three measures of V7, and one measure each of I, V7, and I. The next section uses one measure each of V7, V7, I, I7, IIm, V7, I, I.

### Love Me Do

The Beatles' "Love Me Do" uses the following progression:

```
I7 / / /   | IV / / / | I7 / / /  | IV / / /
I7 / / /   | IV / / / | IV / / /  | IV / / / | IV (break)
I7 / IV / | I / / /  | I7 / IV / | I / / /
```

This whole phrase is repeated and then goes to a bridge which consists of:

```
V / / / | I7 / / / | V / / / | I7 / / /
```

The above phrase is then repeated and the tune returns to the original progression.

### Killer Joe and Twist and Shout

"Killer Joe" uses this two-bar pattern I / IV / | V7 / / / repeated over and over. "Twist and Shout" also uses the same device.

### Yakety Yak

After a seven-beat pickup, this song uses four measures of I, four measures of IV, four measures of V7, and four measures of I.

### Save the Last Dance For Me

This song uses three measures of I, five measures of V7, and two measures of IV, I, V7, and I.

As you can see from the above, if you can master the I, IV, and V7 chords, you can add a great many songs to your repertoire.

# Progressions in the '60s

The '60s were a time of upheaval in society. This was reflected in the music which began to break out of the bounds of earlier forms and progressions. Nevertheless, the I, IV, and V7 chords were still alive and well and the basis of many hit songs of the period. Among them were:

Blowin' in the Wind (Peter, Paul & Mary)
For What It's Worth (Buffalo Springfield) (Uses Only I and IV)
Honky Tonk Woman (Rolling Stones)
King of the Road (Roger Miller)
Like a Rolling Stone (Bob Dylan)
Me and Bobby McGee (Janis Joplin)
Never on Sunday (Movie Theme)
Okie From Muscogee (Merle Haggard)

Papa's Got a Brand New Bag (James Brown)
Respect (Aretha Franklin)
River Deep, Mountain High (Tina Turner)
Satisfaction (Rolling Stones)
Sugar, Sugar (The Archies)
Sweet Caroline (Neil Diamond)
Turn! Turn! Turn! (Pete Seeger)
Watermelon Man (uses all 7th chords: I7, IV7, V7)

## Retrogressions

To the right is the *Circle of 5ths*. As you move counter-clockwise around the circle, each chord is a 4th above the one before it: E, A, D, G, C, F, B♭, E♭, A♭, D♭, F♯, B, and then starting again at E. Because this gives music a feeling of moving forward, we call it a progression. Now, if we play the cycle of 5ths backwards (clockwise), C, G, D, A, E, etc., this is called a *retrogression*. This idea popped up in the '60s, resulting in a new sound that spawned many hits. A lady named Neila Horn composed a tune called "Hey Babe" using five easy guitar chords in a retrogression: C, G, D, A, E. The song was later recorded brilliantly by Jimi Hendrix using the title "Hey Joe."

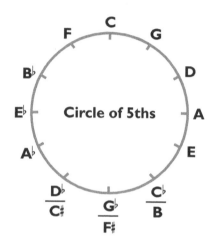

*The "Hey Joe" Retrogression*

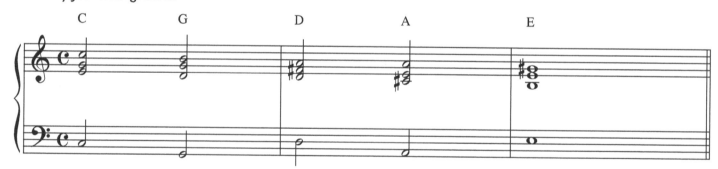

"If I Were a Carpenter" was recorded by Tim Hardin, Johnny Cash, and Bobby Darin. The song also uses a retrogression: I–♭VII–IV–I.

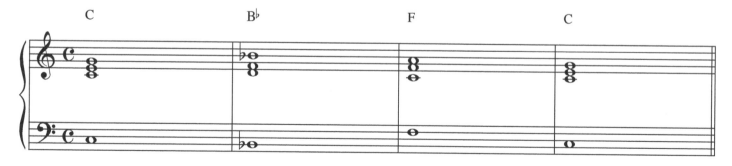

The same sequence is used in the famous fade out of The Beatles' "Hey Jude."

One of the biggest-selling singles of all time was "San Francisco (Be Sure to Wear Some Flowers in Your Hair)." The first phrase is a minor key retrogression: Im–♭VI–♭III–♭VII.

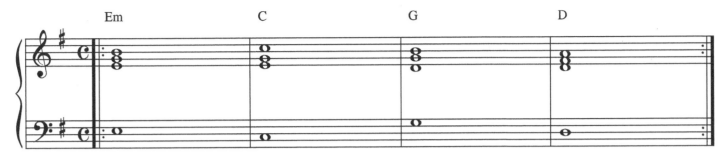

The Beatles' "I Want to Hold Your Hand" uses the retrogression this way:

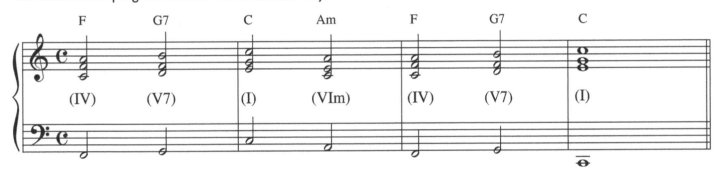

The chords then progress in a more conventional way.

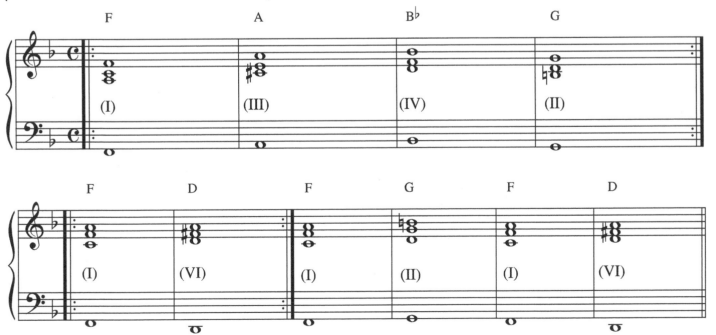

"Sittin' on the Dock of the Bay" is not really a retrogression, but its unique approach to chords places it in this section. All the chords are major triads: I, III, IV, II, and VI.

Another unusual sequence is this one from The Doors' "Light My Fire."

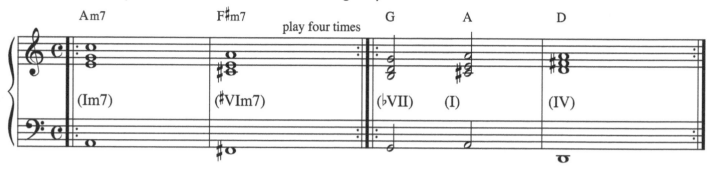

A big hit for Frank Sinatra, "It Was a Very Good Year" moves interestingly between E minor and E major.

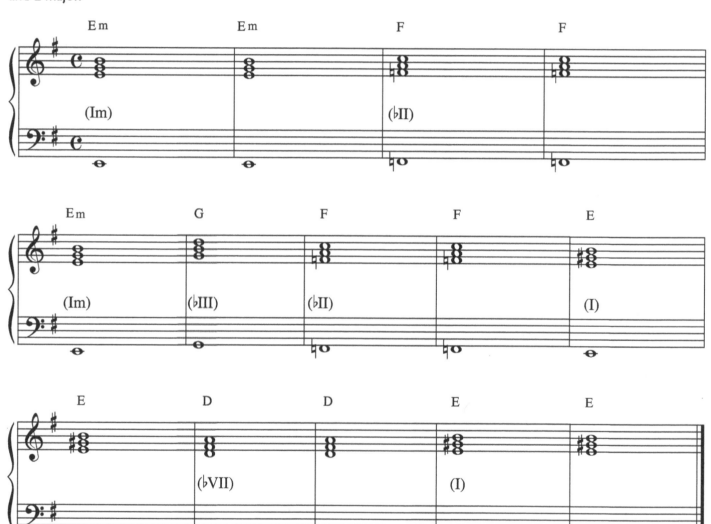

## More Progressions from the '60s

"Eleanor Rigby" is certainly one of the finest songs of the 1960s. The Beatles wrote it using only a I minor chord, with variations Im7 and Im6, and a ♭VI. Here's the progression from the intro:

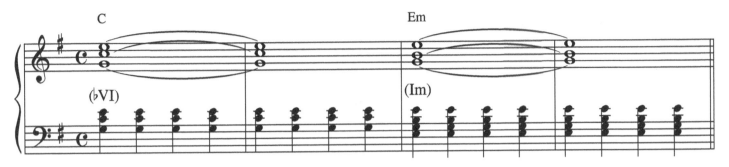

"Sunny" is also in minor key and makes use of Im, ♭III7, ♭VI7, and V7.

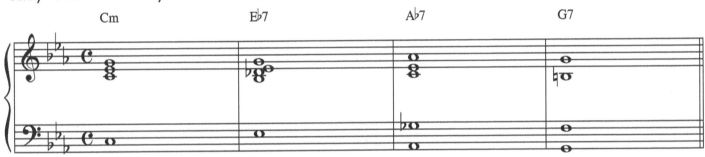

"California Dreamin'" was one of the biggest hits of its decade. Its progression bears studying for its unexpected chords. But notice that the progession's basic motion is from Im (Am) to V (E).

## Lines in the '60s

"The 59th Street Bridge Song," by Paul Simon, uses a two-bar pattern repeated many times. The descending line is a series of 10ths as in the first two bars below. In the last two bars, we've filled in the 10ths to create a more full sound. Notice the use of the G pedal point in the left hand.

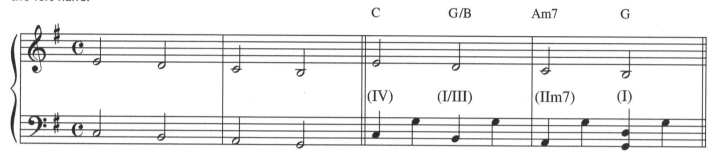

"Mr. Bojangles" was one of the few hits in $\frac{3}{4}$ time. Notice how the line in the bass adds a great deal of interest to what's basically an ordinary progression.

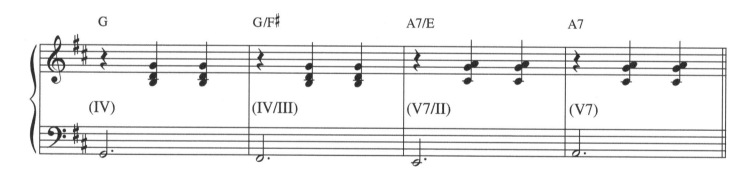

Bob Dylan created "Lay, Lady, Lay" based on a descending chromatic bass line that repeats.

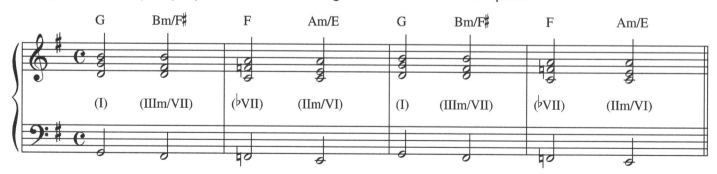

## Some Odds and Ends from the '60s

### These Boots Are Made for Walkin'

Nancy Sinatra's recording of "These Boots Are Made for Walkin'" made quite a splash in the mid-1960s. It featured a smoldering vocal over a very simple progression: eight measures of I, four measures of IV, and four measures of I for the verse (C and F). The chorus alternates between ♭III and I (E♭ and C).

### "Goin' Out of My Head"

This song starts with a very unusual chord and continues through some others until it finally comes to rest on the I chord.

Im7–Imaj7–Im7–Imaj7–IV6–IV6–IIm7–♭VII7–♭III–Vm–♭III–Vm–♭VI–♭VII7–I

In the key of C, this would be:

Cm7–Cmaj7–Cm7–Cmaj7–F6–F6–Dm7–B♭7–E♭–Gm–E♭–Gm–A♭–B♭7–C

### Alice's Restaurant

This song takes a ragtime progression that had been used in "Ja-Da" (1914) and "Walk Right In" (revived in the 1960s) and breathes new life into it. The first eight measures proceed as follows:

| I / / / | VI7 / / / | II7 / V7 / | I / / / | I / / / | VI7 / / / | II7 / / / | V7 / / / |

The four-bar bridge differs in all three songs, but the last four repeat the first four bars.

Quite a few hits from the '60s expanded slightly on the I, IV, V7 progression, often by adding a IIm7. In C, this would be the C, F, and G7 chords with an added Dm7. These would include:

Both Sides Now
Do You Believe In Magic?
Leaving on a Jet Plane (adds a VIm)
For the Good Times (adds I7 and IVm)
It's Not Unusual (adds IIIm)
Puff, the Magic Dragon (adds IIIm and VIm)

# The 1970s and '80s

The 1970s and '80s saw a further expansion of the techniques discussed in this book. Although there still were songs written using only the I, IV, and V7 chords, they became less and less common. The folk music influence became less noticeable, and jazz-influenced players like the Brecker brothers and Steely Dan pushed the limits of chord progressions further into the realm of extended and altered chords. Here are some excerpts of progressions used by many of the outstanding recording artists of the period.

### The Curly Shuffle

This song was an amusing novelty based on a 16-bar blues using only 9th chords: I9, IV9, and V9. In C, this would be eight measures of C9 followed by the usual blues chords: F9, C9, G9, F9, and C9.

### Even the Nights Are Better

Air Supply's recording of the chorus of "Even the Nights Are Better" uses a variation on the I, VIm, IIm, V7 progression that starts on the IIm7.

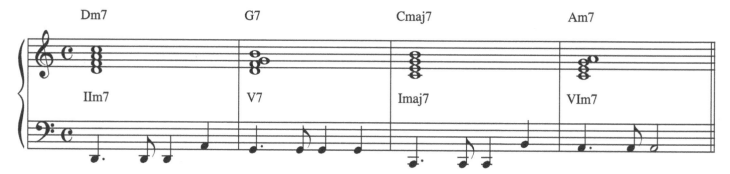

### I Will Survive

Gloria Gaynor had a mega-hit on "I Will Survive." The progression is based on the cycle of 5ths:

### Love Came for Me

This was the love theme from the movie "Splash." It makes extensive use of suspended chords as in the example below.

Notice the important role of variations on I, IV, and V.

## Sesame Street

*Sesame Street* was not only a wonderful, witty children's show, but it also featured a lot of good music, mostly by the late Joe Raposo. In a touching song sung by Kermit the Frog, the melody is supported by an ingenious chord progression based on a descending chromatic bass line, like this.

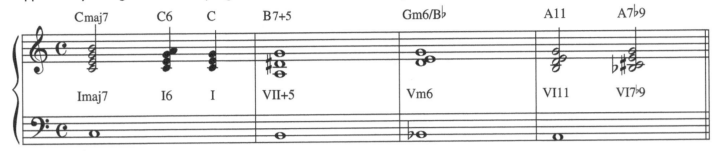

This then resolves using an ordinary IIm7, V7, I.

## Sing

Another song by Joe Raposo, "Sing," uses the keynote of the scale as a pedal point. The first 16 bars of the song, which is in the key of B♭, are played over a B♭ pedal point.

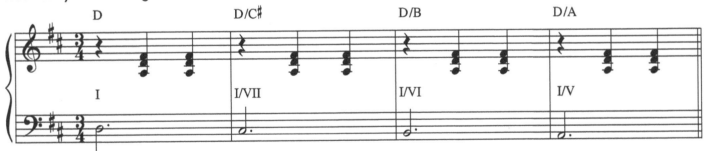

## Annie's Song

Being a guitarist himself, John Denver wrote songs that lie well on the instrument. An example of his writing is "Annie's Song," which features easy guitar chords in the key of D: G, A, Bm, and G, followed by a descending bass line on a D chord.

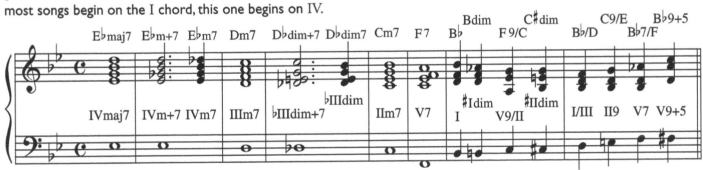

## Candy

Although "Candy" was written back in the '40s, it was revived by The Astors in the '80s with great success. Notice the ingenious bass line, which descends and then rises by step. Although most songs begin on the I chord, this one begins on IV.

76

## Could It Be Magic

In the '70s, Barry Manilow had a hit with "Could It Be Magic," which he adapted from a famous prelude by Frédéric Chopin. The first eight measures make abundant use of suspended chords.

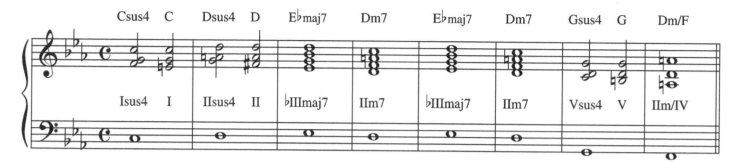

## Hurting Each Other

This was a hit for The Carpenters. The first eight measures illustrate the use of a tonic pedal point. (The tonic is the note that names the key, in this case, C.)

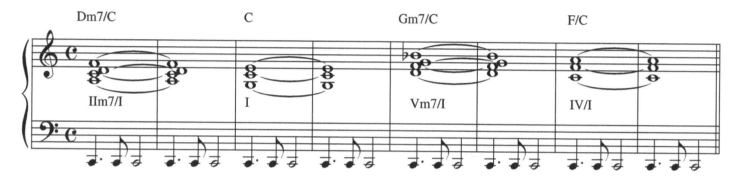

## I'm Sorry

John Denver had many hits during this time. In "I'm Sorry," he used a bass line constructed from a series of easy guitar chords.

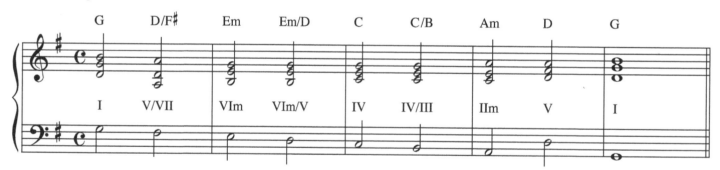

## Love Will Keep Us Together

Measures 11–14 of The Captain and Tennille's "Love Will Keep Us Together" illustrate the use of a rising chromatic line that connects four F chords.

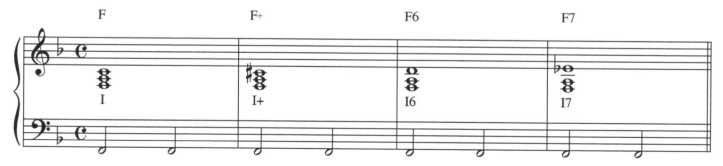

The progression then proceeds through IV–I–IV/V, and back to I.

## My Sweet Lady

John Denver, who became a pop superstar in the '70s, was quite a good guitarist in the folk style. He worked out many of his progressions on the guitar, as, for example, his lovely ballad "My Sweet Lady." Guitarists would tune the 6th string down to a D, and this note is repeated throughout the first six measures before proceeding through the usual IIm and V chords to return to the beginning.

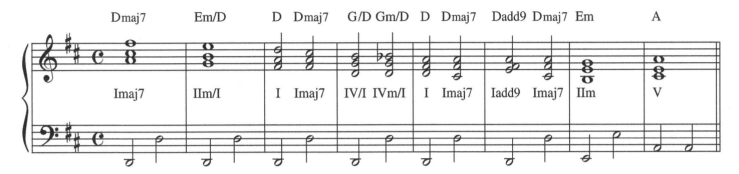

## The Rainbow Connection

The Muppet Movie introduced this song. Although the progression is basically I–VIm–IIm–V7, notice how variations (in gray) give it a thoroughly modern sound.

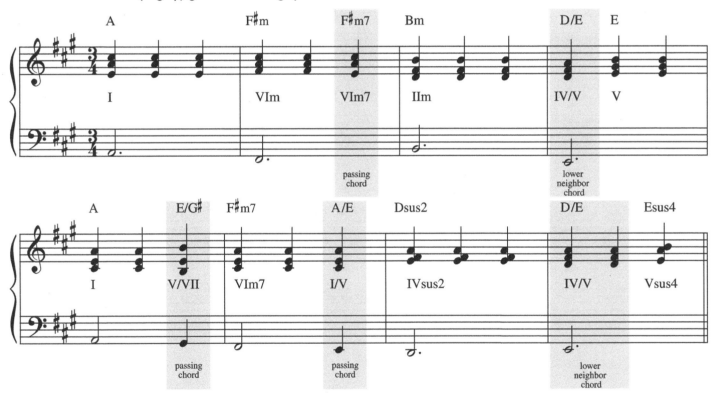

## You Make Me Feel Brand New

The Stylistics were one of the finest vocal groups of the '70s. In their hit "You Make Me Feel Brand New," the arrangement teeters between E major and G major. First, a series of chords in E major are heard: I–IVm–I–IVm–I–VIm7–II7–VII–I. Then, after two chords announce the new key of G (IV and V), we hear a similar progression in the new key: I–IVm–I–IVm–I–IVm–I, followed by a fairly conventional progression in G. Later, the song returns to the key of E and eventually fades out in the key of G.

78

## You Are Everything

Another hit for The Stylistics, "You Are Everything," also features key changes and the following
figure, which has been around a long time. Many examples of it can be found in the music of
J. S. Bach from 300 years ago! This excerpt is from the chorus and is repeated three times.

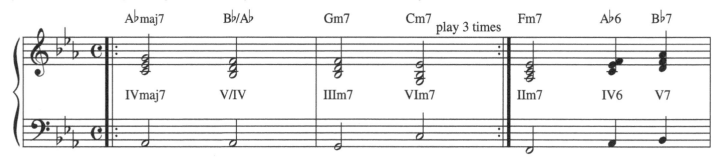

And just when it sounds as though the progression is finally headed toward the I chord of E♭, it
makes a surprising change of key to C, then F, and finally ends in B♭.

## Truly

Lionel Richie had many hits during the 1970s and '80s. Among them was "Truly," which is
notable for its ingenious chromatic bass lines. This is a transposition of the progression to C
from its original D-flat.

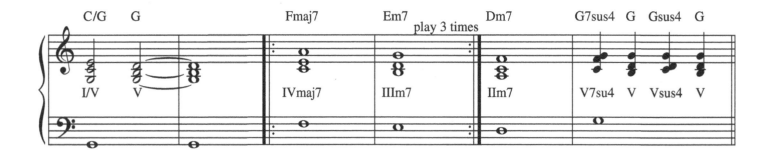

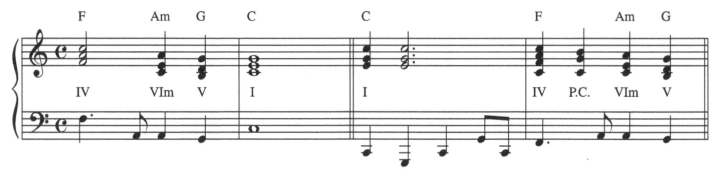

## Badlands

In this progression, Bruce Springsteen uses only the I, IV, and V7 chords, except for a few
spots where he inserts some passing chords. We've transposed the tune to C major from the
original E major.

## Beautiful Noise

Neil Diamond's "Beautiful Noise" consists of two main sections, one in D and the other in C. Besides the usual I, IV, and V chords, the D section touches on fairly remote chords, including ♭VII (C and C7) and ♭III (F). The C section sticks to the I, IV, and V7 chords in the new key.

## Bennie and the Jets

Elton John can always be counted on for interesting progressions, and "Bennie and the Jets" is no exception. The intro sets up the key of G, and the progression starts on the IIm7 in measure 5.

## Black Dog

Led Zeppelin's "Black Dog" is built mostly over a moving bass line without using chords at all. When chords are used, however, they are (in the key of A) I (A), ♭III (C), ♭VII (G), and IV (D). It's very unusual to hear a song that never gets to the V chord, but it certainly works in this one.

## FM

Steely Dan is composed of two former jazz musicians who use many altered and extended chords. In their composition "FM," you'll find IV/V, major 7ths, 6/9, 13ths, m7♭5, minor 9ths, and 7♯5 chords. After seven measures of Em7 and A7, we hear the following series of diatonic and chromatic passing chords.

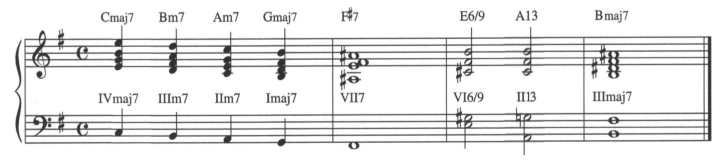

### Crocodile Rock

The intro to Elton John's "Crocodile Rock" shows what can be done with standard progressions I–IV–V and I–VIm–IV–V.

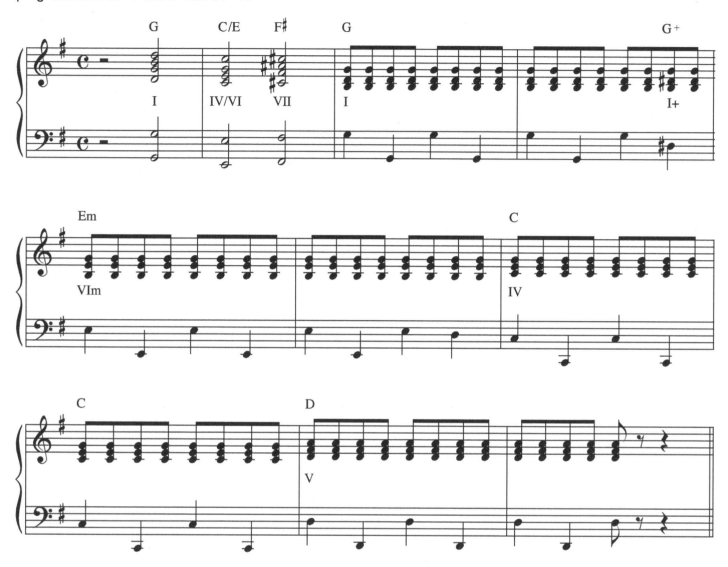

Especially take note of the F♯ chord in measure 2, which replaces the expected D chord. In measure 4, the G+ is a chromatic passing chord between G and Em.

### Fifty Ways to Leave Your Lover

Paul Simon was responsible for many hit songs in the '70s and '80s. In "Fifty Ways to Leave Your Lover," besides the witty lyric, he has a few progressions that merit attention. The sequence Im–♭VII–♭VI–V7 is often associated with Spanish flamenco music, but here Simon shows how it can be used in a completely different context.

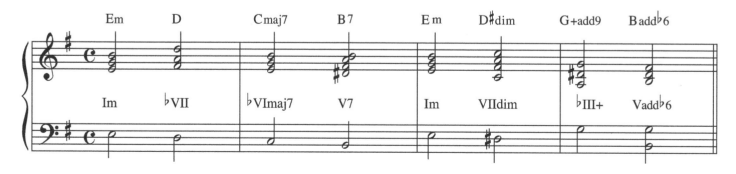

## *Life in the Fast Lane*

The Eagles have been responsible for many rock classics, including "Life in the Fast Lane." The song is built on the I, IV7, and V7 chords in the key of E (E, A7, and B7). In the coda (the last 10 measures), however, they make ingenious use of an E pedal point.

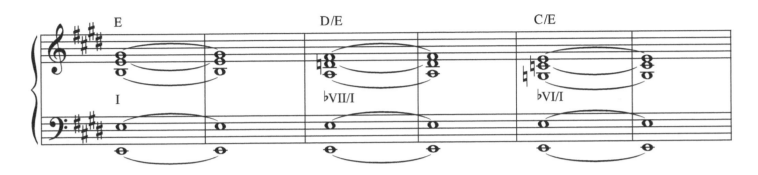

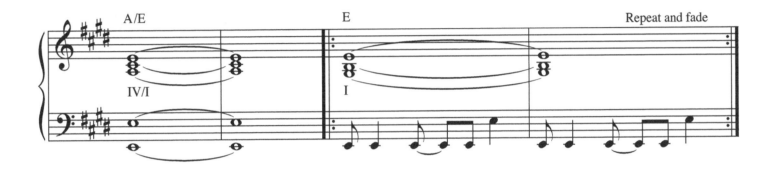

## *You're in My Heart*

In Rod Stewart's "You're in My Heart," the following four-bar sequence is repeated many times. The progression is transposed up a half step to C from the original B major.

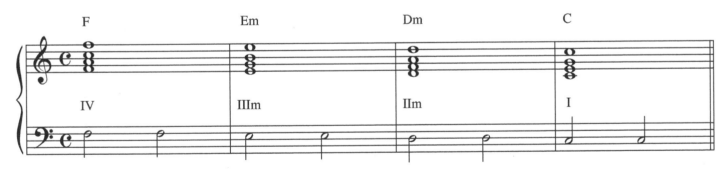

# Rock Standards

## Gimme Some Lovin'

Stevie Winwood's "Gimme Some Lovin'" (in the key of E) is another example of a tune that avoids the V or V7 chord. The intro is built on an E pedal using D/E–A/E–E–E7. The verse continues the E pedal, using two beats of E and two beats of A/E, and this pattern is repeated eight times. The chorus is the four bars below followed by a return to the E–A/E pattern.

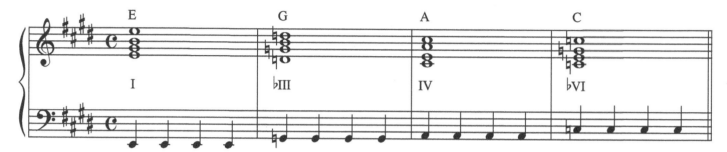

## Heartbreaker

The chorus of Pat Benatar's "Heartbreaker" starts out with power chords in the key of F minor.

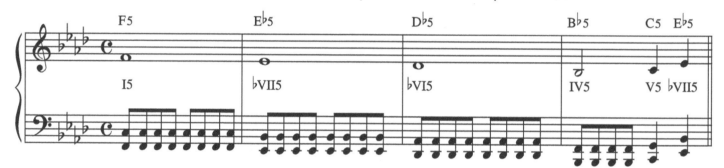

## Shelter from the Storm

Three-chord songs can still be hits. However, in Bob Dylan's "Shelter from the Storm," the chords are not I, IV, and V7 as might be expected, but I, IIIm, and IV (D, F#m, and G in the key of D).

## Margaritaville

Jimmy Buffett's "Margaritaville" uses only four chords: I, IV, V7, and I7 in the key of D.

## Lyin' Eyes

The Eagles use five chords in the verse of their mega-hit "Lyin' Eyes." They are I (G), Imaj7 (Gmaj7), IV (C), IIm (Am), and V (D), a variation on the standard I–VIm–IIm–V7 progression.

## "Sly" Progression

Sly and the Family Stone used an ordinary progression in the key of F, but avoided the I chord completely, using a VIm (Dm) instead.

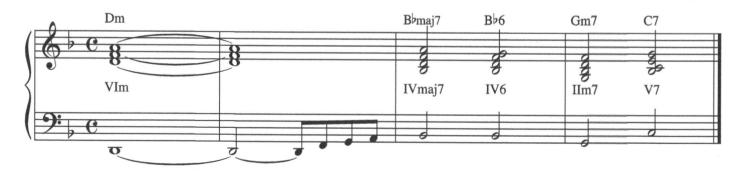

## Stairway to Heaven

Led Zeppelin started the '70s with "Stairway to Heaven," one of the biggest-selling records of all time. The theme is based on variations of the A minor chord.

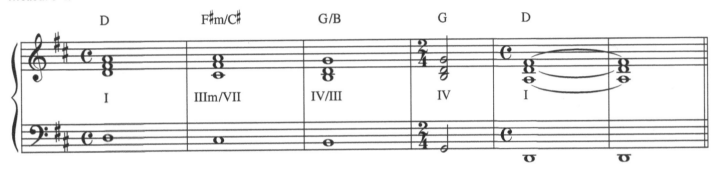

## Forever Young

Bob Dylan's "Forever Young" begins with this interesting progression. Notice the $\frac{2}{4}$ bar in measure 4.

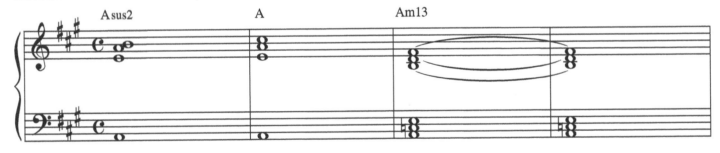

## Blue

Joni Mitchell wrote this classic in 1973. It's in the key of A and uses I (A), IV (D), ♭III (C), ♭VII (G), and ♭VI (F) in the verse. The chorus uses many of these chords plus an Asus4. Later on in the chorus, we hear this unusual sequence:

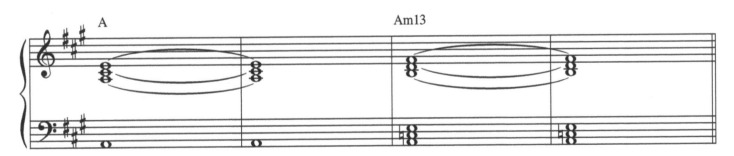

## *Don't Worry, Be Happy*

Bobby McFerrin is certainly one of the most talented performers on the music scene. He had a huge hit with "Don't Worry, Be Happy," recorded in the unusual key of B major and using only three chords, I (B) , IIm (C#m), and IV (E).

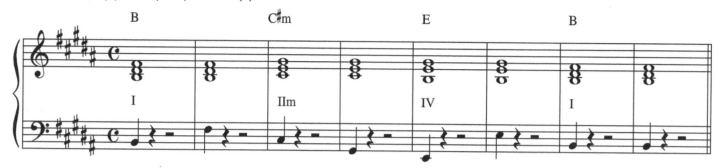

## *The Way it Is*

Bruce Hornsby's "The Way It Is" makes extensive use of the progression below. Notice the melodic pedal point on II (A).

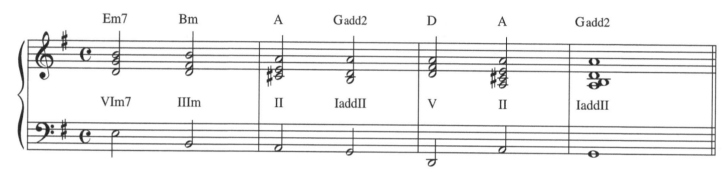

# The 1990s

The 1990s saw further development of popular chord progressions. As more and more trained musicians entered the pop field, we got to hear more and more modern techniques, such as suspended chords, extended and altered chords, power chords, pedal points, and others.

## Heart of the Matter

Don Henley's "Heart of the Matter" began the decade with this example of a melodic pedal point. Notice how the note B, the 5th of the key of E, is repeated as the chords change, while the bass line moves up by step.

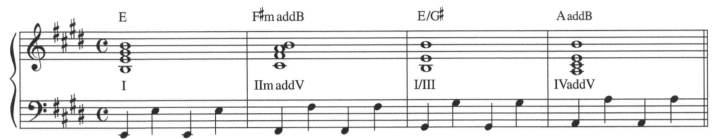

## River of Dreams

Billy Joel's "River of Dreams" begins with an ordinary I–IV–V progression in E, but then moves in some unexpected directions. And notice the unusual melodic pedal point on G# (the 7th of the scale) contrasted with the descending stepwise bass line.

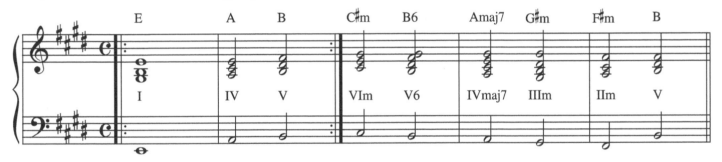

## Smells Like Teen Spirit

Nirvana recorded "Smells Like Teen Spirit" in the early 1990s. Kurt Cobain's searing vocal comes in over a repeated figure based on four power chords. Notice that the V chord is completely avoided.

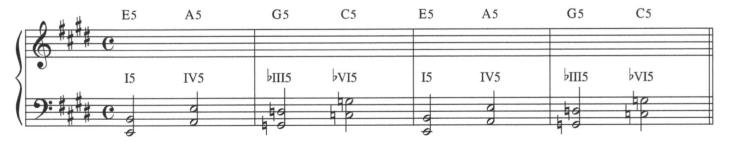

### Walking in Memphis

The 1991 hit "Walking in Memphis" used a repeated four-bar progression.

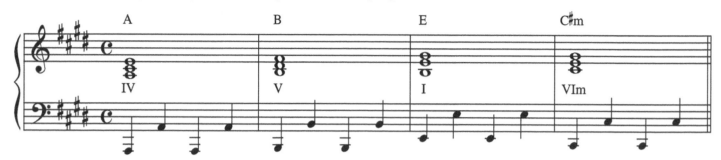

### My Heart Will Go On

Celine Dion recorded the theme from "Titanic" in 1997. The song, called "My Heart Will Go On," is in the key of F, but the *cadence* (the resolution of the phrase back to the I chord) is delayed for many measures.

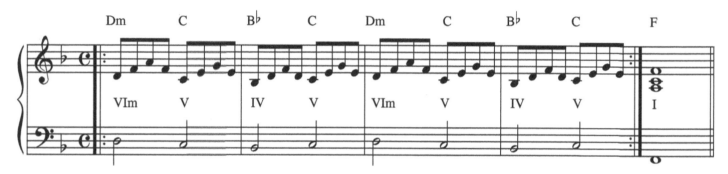

# The 2000s

Continuing the trend that we have seen in previous decades, we notice the prevalence of chords using suspensions and alternate bass notes. Power chords and pedal points also play an important role in today's music. Here are a few examples of progressions that were popular in this decade.

## Beautiful
"Beautiful," by Linda Perry, was a big hit for Christina Aguilera. The first four chords are built on a descending bass line. The key is E♭.

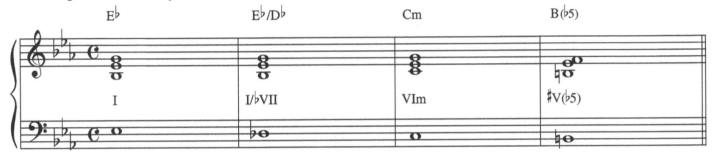

Later in the song, we hear these chords. The sequence is then repeated.

## Breathe
"Breathe," by Holly Lamar and Stephanie Bentley, was a big hit for Faith Hill in 2000. Notice how the stepwise motion in the bass gives an ordinary progression extra vitality.

## Complicated
"Complicated," by Avril Lavigne, uses a variation on the I–VIm–IV–V7 progression in F.

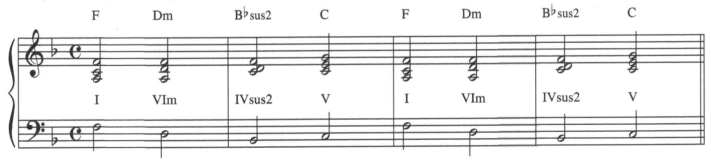

When we get to the bridge of "Complicated," we hear several power chords.

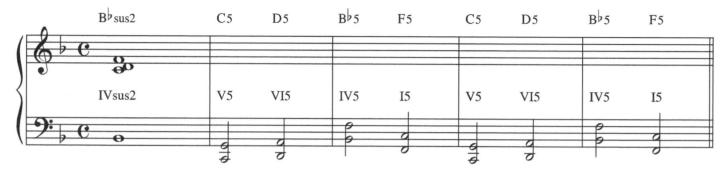

## Don't Know Why

"Don't Know Why," by Jesse Harris, was a hit for Norah Jones in 2002. This progression, which is in the key of B♭, uses many suspensions, extensions, and passing chords.

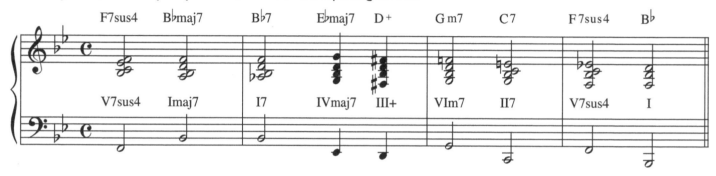

## Fallen

"Fallen," by Sarah McLachlan, is in D minor and uses the following chords:

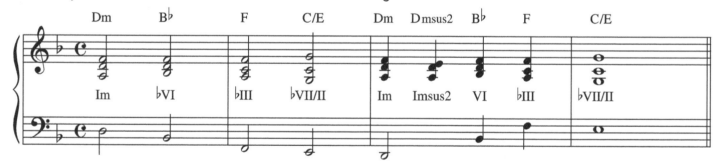

## Get the Party Started

Pink is one of the biggest-selling artists today. Her recording of Linda Perry's "Get the Party Started" uses a B minor chord for many measures, sometimes with a sus2 (Bmsus2).

## Hey Ya!

André Benjamin (a.k.a. André 3000), one of the duo OutKast, had a hit with this progression in 2004. The song, "Hey Ya!" moves between G major and E major or minor. The first four chords are repeated many times, then the last four chords are played.

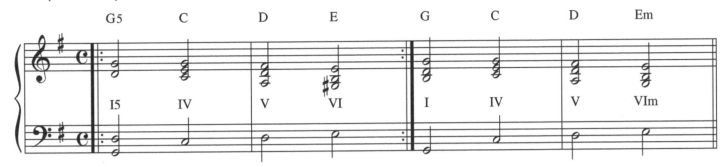

## Jenny from the Block

The song "Jenny from the Block" (2004), recorded by Jennifer Lopez, is based on an interesting descending bass line.

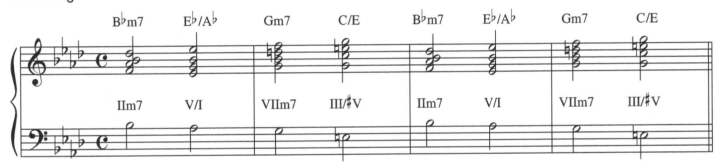

## Underneath Your Clothes

Shakira recorded "Underneath Your Clothes" in 2002. The tune is in F minor, and notice how the stepwise motion in the bass adds interest and coherence to the whole progression.

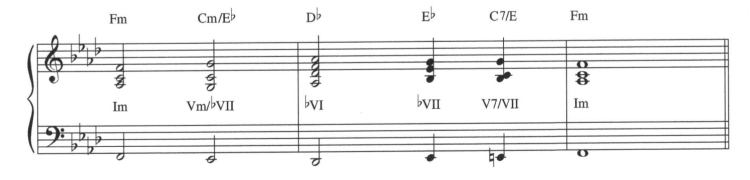

### The Space Between Us

The Dave Mathews Band can always be counted on for interesting progressions and powerful songs. "The Space Between Us" is in A major. The song begins with an interesting combination of power chords and a pedal point.

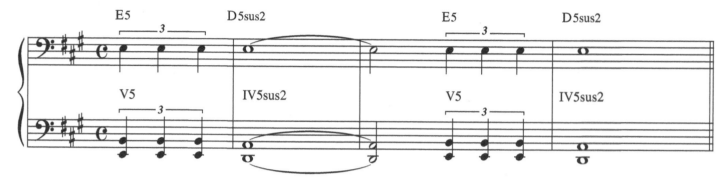

Later in the song, a stepwise bass line adds interest to an ordinary chord progression.

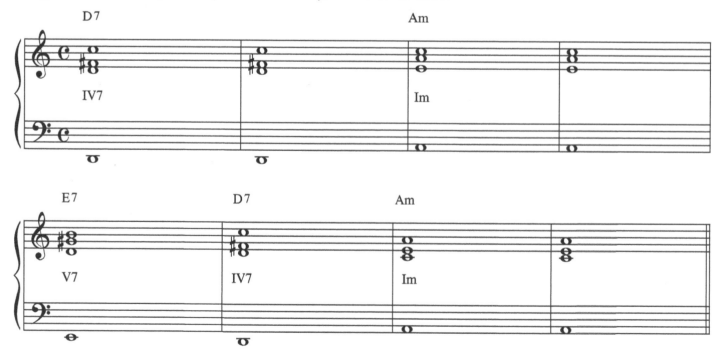

---

# More Classic Songs

---

### Gotta Serve Somebody

Bob Dylan shows his folk-rock roots in a three-chord song called "Gotta Serve Somebody." After an eight-bar verse entirely on Am (the I minor chord), the chorus continues.

### Already Gone

Often, interest can be added to an ordinary I–IV–V7 progression by changing the key. The Eagles did this in their hit "Already Gone," which starts by using the I, IV, and V chords in the key of G, and then shifts to the key of C and uses the I, IV, and V chords in that key.

### Badlands

Although Bruce Springsteen's "Badlands" features a few variations, the basic progression consists of our old friends, the I, IV, and V (or V7) chords in the key of E.

### Barracuda

Heart's "Barracuda" sticks to major triads, but gets a lot of mileage from them. There are also many meter changes from $\frac{4}{4}$ to $\frac{3}{4}$ to $\frac{2}{4}$. The key is E major. After a long section that uses the I and ♭VI chords (E and C), the song continues.

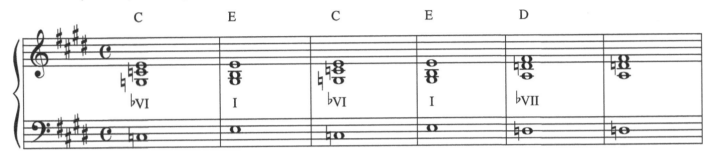

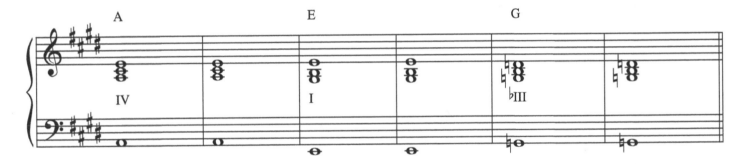

### I Can't Tell You Why

In the Eagles' song "I Can't Tell You Why," they begin the song on the I and IV chords, but use major 7ths instead of triads for a more emotional sound. The key is D major. Interestingly, this is the same progression used in Erik Satie's famous "Gymnopédie No. 1."

# SECTION 4
# CHORD SUBSTITUTIONS

## Substitutions

In modern jazz, it's standard practice to avoid plain major, minor, diminished, and augmented triads, as well as dominant 7th chords. Following are substitutions that can be used for the major I, the minor I, and the V7 chords.

### For a Major I Chord

| Substitute | Spelled in the Key of C | Comments |
|---|---|---|
| Isus9 also called Isus2 | D–E–G | D takes the place of C |
| Isus4 | C–F–G | |
| I6 | C–E–G–A | |
| Imaj7 | C–E–G–B | |
| I6/9 | C–E–G–A–D | |
| Imaj9 | C–E–G–B–D | |
| I6/9#11 | C–E–G–A–D–F# | |
| Imaj9#11 | C–E–G–B–D–F# | |
| Imaj13 | C–E–G–B–D–(F#)–A | You can include or omit the F#. |
| IIIm7 | E–G–B–D | Because it contains the same notes as the upper part of a Imaj9 (C–E–G–B–D) |
| VIm7 | A–C–E–G | Because it contains the same notes as I6 (C–E–G–A) |

Make up your own variations. Almost any combination of the root, 3rd, 5th, 6th, major 7th, 9th, sharped 11th, and 13th can be used.

### For a Minor I Chord

| | | |
|---|---|---|
| Imsus2 also called Imsus9 | D–E♭–G | The D takes the place of the C |
| Imsus4 | C–F–G | |
| Im6 | C–E♭–G–A | |
| Im+7 | C–E♭–G–B | |
| Im6/9 | C–E♭–G–A–D | |
| Im+7+9 | C–E♭–G–B–D | |
| Im+11 | C–E♭–G–B–D–F | For another variation, use F# instead of F in this chord. |
| Im13+7+9 | C–E♭–G–B–D–(F or F#)–A | |

Make up your own variations. Almost any combination of the root, flat 3rd, 5th, 6th, major7th, 9th, 11th or sharped 11th, and 13th can be used.

### For a V7 (Seventh) Chord

| | | |
|---|---|---|
| V9 | G–B–D–F–A | |
| V11 | G–B–D–F–A–C | |
| V13 | G–B–D–F–A–(C)–E | The 11th is usually omitted in this chord |

Various notes—especially the 5th and 9th—can be altered:

| | | | |
|---|---|---|---|
| V7♭9 | G–B–D–F–A♭ | V9♭5 | G–B–D♭–F–A |
| V7#9 | G–B–D–F–A# or B♭ | V7♭5♭9 | G–B–D♭–F–A♭ |
| V+11 | G–B–D–F–A–C# | V7♭5♯9 | G–B–D♭–F–A# or B♭ |
| V13+11 | G–B–D–F–A–C#–E | V7#5♭9 | G–B–D#–F–A♭ |
| V7♭5 | G–B–D♭–F | V7#5♯9 | G–B–D#–F–A# |
| V7#5 | G–B–D#–F | | |

Or, make up your own variations. Virtually any combination of sharped, flatted or natural 5ths, 9ths, 11ths, and 13ths will work, as long as the 3rd and ♭7 (B and F) are left undisturbed.

## The Tritone Substitution

The ♭II7 chord is a tritone (six half steps) away from the V7 chord. In the key of C, the ♭II7 chord is D♭7 and the V7 is G7. From D♭ to G is a tritone, three whole steps: D♭ to E♭, E♭ to F, and F to G. If you start with G, you still get three whole steps: G to A, A to B, B to C♯ or D♭. We know that the tritone in the G7 chord is B–F. If we look at the tritone in the D♭7 chord, we see that it is F to C♭. Since C♭ is the same note as B, we can see that both G7 and D♭7 share the same tritone. Therefore, the D♭7 chord can substitute for the G7 in virtually every case where it doesn't clash with the melody. Not only that, but all the substitutes for the V7 chord described above can be used as ♭II7 chords. For example, instead of G9♭5, use D♭9♭5. Instead of G13♭9, use D♭13♭9, and so on.

---

*Example*

In a progression that goes IIm7 / V7 / | IIm7 / V7 / (Dm7 / G7 / | Dm7 / G7 / ) you could play…

IIm7 / V7 / | IIm7 / ♭II7 / (Dm7 / G7 / | Dm7 / D♭7 / )

…and of course you can use any extensions of, or substitutions for, the chords such as:

IIm9 / V13 / | IIm11 / ♭II+11 / (Dm9 / G13 / | Dm11 / D♭aug11 / ).

---

Using the tritone substitute (♭II7) for the V7 chord yields interesting variations for endings.

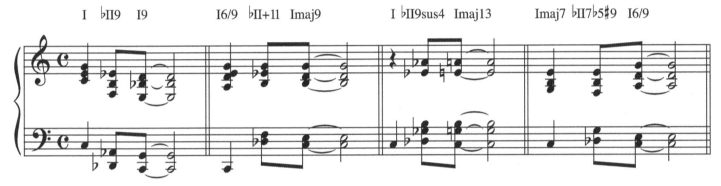

## How to Avoid the Tritone Within a Chord

Most modern players and arrangers prefer avoiding the tritone; in a G7, the tritone is B–F, the 3rd and flatted 7th of the chord. One way to avoid it is to substitute the 4th for the 3rd of the chord.

If the V7 chord is played for eight beats, the progression may be made more interesting by preceding the V7 with a IIm7 chord:

Instead of Dm7, you could use a Dm9, a Dm11, or a Dm13 chord. Any of the substitutes for the G7 which avoid the tritone (see above) can be used for the last four beats. Here are a few examples that can be found in rock standards:

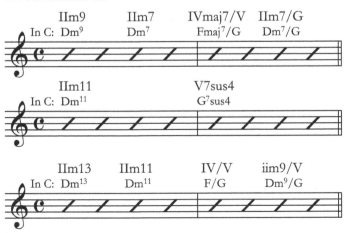

Using altered notes:

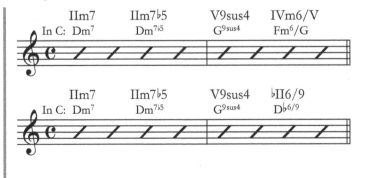

The preceding material illustrates the dozens, perhaps, hundreds of ways the V7 chord may be used. But always keep in mind the style of music you're playing. If you're playing folk music or polkas, pretty much stick to basic triads and 7th chords. For traditional jazz and country music, add diminished and augmented chords and an occasional 7th. In modern pop and show tunes, all the chords you've learned are appropriate. Modern jazz players make it a point to avoid triads of any kind, so all the extensions and alterations we've discussed will come in handy. In rock, pretty much stay away from any dominant 7ths, 11ths, and 13ths, although major 7ths, minor 7ths, major 6ths, minor 6ths, suspended chords, and chords with alternate bass notes are okay.

## Diminished Chords

First, you should understand that there are only three different diminished chords: C–E♭–F♯–A, C♯(D♭)–E–G–B♭, and D–F–A♭(G♯)–B. Each chord can be named for any of the notes in it. The first chord listed can be called C diminished, E♭ diminished, F♯ diminished, or A diminished. The second chord can be called C♯ (or D♭) diminished, E diminished, G diminished, or B♭ diminished. The last chord can be called D diminished, F diminished, A♭ (or G♯) diminished, or B diminished. Some may fuss about spelling, but what's listed above is the usual way these chords are seen.

Diminished chords contain not one but two tritones. For example, C diminished is spelled C–E♭–F♯–A. From C to F♯ is a tritone, and so is E♭ to A. Any diminished chord can be extended by adding a major 7th, a major 9th, or an 11th, or any combination of these.

## Avoiding the Tritone in Diminished Chords

Now, here's a very useful thing to notice: If you lower any note in a diminished chord you wind up with a dominant 7th chord. For example, let's start with C diminished. Lower the C a half step to B. This leads to a chord spelled B–E♭(D♯)–F♯–A, an ordinary B7 chord. Try another note: Lower the E♭ to D. Now you have D–F♯–A–C, which is a D7. If you lower the F♯ to F you get an F7. Lowering the A to A♭ gives you an A♭7. These four chords, B7, D7, F7, and A♭7, can be used as substitutes for the C diminished chord. And (since 7th chords still contain one tritone) you can use all the substitutes for seventh chords that we've already discussed. If you like the tritone sound, use those substitutes. If you don't, use the techniques you've learned to avoid the tritone. Since the tritone sound is out of favor at the moment, here are a few ways to avoid it in diminished chords:

Basic progression:

Avoiding the Tritone:

Using IIIm7 instead of I allows for a nice side-slipping progression (see page 32). Please note that IIIm7 is like the top part of a Imaj9 chord and so can substitute for the I chord. Em7=E–G–B–D substitutes for Cmaj9 = C–E–G–B–D. The Beatles used this exact progression (in the key of E but transposed to the key of C here) for their ballad "Do You Want to Know a Secret."

Keeping to the basic progression of I / Idim / IIm7 / V7 / (C / Cdim / Dm7 / G7 / ), we can use the IV7 as a substitute for Idim. Notice that the tritone is avoided.

The II7 sometimes can be used for the Idim as in this example:

## Substituting for Augmented Chords

All augmented chords, including augmented triads, 7#5s, and 9#5s, can be thought of as belonging to one of two *whole tone* scales. As the name implies, a whole tone scale is a scale consisting of only whole steps (there are no half steps as in major scales). There are only two possible whole tone scales:

$$C–D–E–F\sharp(or\ G\flat)–G\sharp(or A\flat)–B\flat\ (or A\sharp) \quad or \quad C\sharp(or\ D\flat)–E\flat–F–G–A–B$$

As you can see, the C+ or C augmented triad (C–E–G♯) belongs to the first scale. If we add the 7th or B♭, and/or the 9th or D, we still have only added notes belonging to this scale. Additionally, we can see that the ♭5 (G♭) also belongs to this scale, which means chords like C7♭5, C9♭5, and C+11(omit 5th) also belong to the scale and can substitute for Caug. From this we can conclude that any chord that contains only the notes from a whole tone scale can substitute for any other chord from the same scale. For example, C+ can not only substitute for E+ and G♯+, but also for C7♯5, C7♭5, C9♯5, C9♭5, and so on.

## Tonicization (ton-nic-iz-AY-shun or ton-nih-size-AY-shun)

This is a fancy word for a simple technique. It means to treat a new chord like a new key. Let's say the progression is:

Instead of treating the Am as a chord in the key of C, treat it as the temporary new key of Am. Since the V7 to I is the basic chord change in all keys, this might suggest that you use a III7 (E7) to get to the VIm (Am). The new version of the progression might be:

Now you can use any of the substitutes for the E7 that you have learned (see pages 92–94). If you use the tritone substitute for III7, which is ♭VII7 (B♭7), you can use all those substitutes, as well.

If the basic progression is I to IIIm (C to Em), you could use a VII7 chord to get there.

You can use the tonicization technique even if the new chord is not in the key, like the B♭ chord in this example:

The opening measures of "Over the Rainbow" can serve as an illustration. In the key of C, the first two measures are C / Am / Em / C7. The substitute version could be: C / B7♭9 / Em / / C7. Even better, you can insert a IIm7♭5 before the V7♭9 in the new (temporary) key of E minor: C / F♯m7♭5 B7♭9 Em / / C7. And as usual, you can use any of the substitutes you've learned for the Em and C7 chords.

Using a similar technique, you can substitute for the I to IV progression by treating the IV as a new key:

Treat the F chord as the key of F and you can enter it using IIm7–V7 (Gm7–C7) in the new key to get to it.

You can use this on any blues tune when the chord changes from I to IV.

Basic progression:

Tonicize IV:

You can use the tonicization technique even if the new chord is not in the key, as in this example from the jazz standard "Three Little Words."

Basic progression:

Treat the A♭9 as the new key of A♭, and you could approach it with an E♭9 chord, using the usual substitutes:

Tonicize A♭:

Since you can then tonicize the substitutes, this technique can be taken to absurd lengths, so we advise you to use it with taste and discretion.

Here is an example of turnarounds using substitutions.

Using tritone substitutes:

Using tonicization to keep the chords changing every beat:

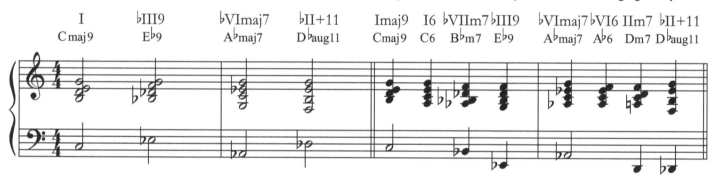

Since the IIIm7 chord (E–G–B–D) contains the same notes as the upper part of Imaj9 (C–E–G–B–D), we can use it as a substitute. This suggests turnarounds like these two:

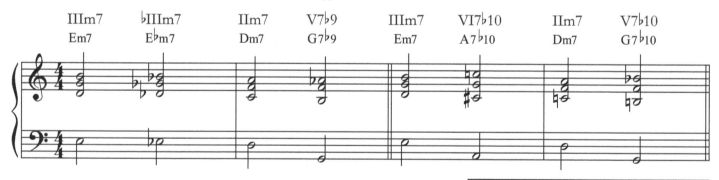

Note: ♭10 is an alternate spelling of ♯9

## A Final Word

There are two things that will greatly assist you in expanding your musical horizons. The more you play with other musicians, the better you will be able to identify which chord progressions work well with each other's instruments, and which ones seem overly complex and unpleasant to listen to. Recording your own playing is a tremendous help, and with the current availability of cheap recording gear and computer-based recording systems, recording your playing no longer requires renting a recording studio. Have fun, and we encourage you to come up with your own chord progressions and variations.

DF DW